I hope that you
will enjoy our
adoption story!

Roger Bowling

May these words
be a blessing to
your heart & soul!

_Natalie
Bowling_

Dear Lois

Our Adoption Journey

KAREN SCHLINDWEIN &
AMALIE BOWLING

WESTBOW®
PRESS
A DIVISION OF THOMAS NELSON
& ZONDERVAN

WestBow Press books may be ordered through booksellers or by contacting:

WestBow Press
A Division of Thomas Nelson & Zondervan
1663 Liberty Drive
Bloomington, IN 47403
www.westbowpress.com
1 (866) 928-1240

ISBN: 978-1-4908-7532-3 (sc)
ISBN: 978-1-4908-7533-0 (hc)
ISBN: 978-1-4908-7531-6 (e)

Library of Congress Control Number: 2015905132

Print information available on the last page.

WestBow Press rev. date: 05/07/2015

DEDICATION

This book is dedicated to Lois and Ruth, who conceived, chose life for, and nurtured Amalie and Joseph and chose to knit our family together. Because of their selfless love, our empty arms were filled, and we became the family we had dreamed of for so long. Their decisions impacted many lives, and we thank our Lord that their model of sacrificial love has greatly affected who we are and how we've tried to live our lives.

ACKNOWLEDGMENTS

All thanks to our Lord and Savior, Jesus Christ, for dying on the cross for our sins and paving a path for our eternal life. Our faith is what we lean on and is the foundation of who we are. We are thankful for our husbands, Tom and Jason, whom God chose for us and whose unconditional love and encouragement have helped us to write this book. To Joe, our son and brother: we love you for who you are, *as you are*, and pray that you will recognize the plans God has for you, as He declares in your life verse (Jer. 29:11).

Bryan, Jenaya and families, we are so blessed to have you as part of our family and are excited to be on the journey we now travel together! To our family and friends who have supported and encouraged us through this project we are grateful for your prayers and for cheering us on. We are especially thankful to our contributors (Tom, Jason, Joe, Nana Lillian, Papa Walt, Grandma Midge, Liz, Kim, Bryan, Jenaya, and Pat) who helped to weave the story together.

Thank you to my (Karen's) daddy for letting me read this book to you as it was being written. Though your mind doesn't always remember and your thoughts are hard to express, your encouragement during our times of reading together was inspiring and motivated me to finish.

We are so appreciative of our editing team (Laurie, Linda, Ann, and Lori); your time, comments, and encouragement were priceless to us. A very special thanks also goes to Steph, who was the first to hear about the idea for this book and encouraged me (Karen) to reach from within and find the confidence and courage to pursue the dream of sharing our story. Thank you for believing in me more than I believed in myself.

Preface (Karen)

Trust in the Lord with all your heart and lean
not on your own understanding; in all your ways
submit to him, and he will make your paths
straight. —Proverbs 3:5–6 (NIV)

As a young married woman in my mid-twenties, I wish that this verse from Proverbs was something I had understood. Instead, God chose to teach me the meaning of trusting Him through the journey of adoption. What a journey it has been!

Since I had grown up as an only child, God had already prepared me to open my heart to adoption. My parents wanted to have more children, but that wasn't in God's plan. So they chose to give of themselves for several years as foster parents. We had many babies who came into our lives—some for a very short time, most for a few months, and our first for over a year. Our role as a family was to nurture them until a loving family adopted them. I was blessed to experience adoption firsthand; God had planted a seed in my life.

Many years later, when my husband and I decided to start a family, a still-small voice told me we would have challenges. At the time, the voice wasn't clear to me, and we began a journey on which we faced many difficult days. Infertility treatment began, and sheer stubbornness and drive caused us to forge ahead through each month of disappointment, sometimes more heartbreaking than the previous month, until we finally became pregnant. I was so sure that this baby was going to be the answer to fill my lonely heart. But two months later, we miscarried, and I thought life couldn't get much worse.

Because we were both open to adoption we sent out a plea to our family and friends, asking them to keep us in mind if they became aware of an adoptive situation. Within a few weeks came the first call that changed the course of our lives forever. A family member's close friend was ready to deliver a baby; she already had two children and didn't feel she could parent the new baby. Within a couple of days, we met her, and she immediately chose us to be her baby's parents. Sixteen short days later, she blessed us with the privilege of watching our daughter, Amalie, be born into this world; it was the first time in my life that I gave pause to God's goodness. There was nothing else that could explain to me the selfless sacrifice of a wonderful birth mother who'd placed her baby's needs over her own. The next day, she placed this beautiful baby into our arms and told us to have a good life with her, to love her, and to be her parents.

Two and a half years later, through the selflessness of another birth mother, our son, Joseph, was born into our lives. Our earthly family was complete! And yet, as beautiful as this family was, something was still missing …

Because of a job transfer, we moved from Minnesota to Wisconsin and within a short time joined a Bible study group, where we wrestled with the message of salvation we'd heard. When we finally grasped and accepted God's gift of grace, we became believers in Christ. God immediately blessed me by allowing me to colead an infertility and adoption ministry for several years at our church. It was a time in my life that gave me great joy, as I was able to help others during a dark and challenging time in their lives.

Amalie ("Mali") and Joseph ("Joe") have known about their adoptions since they could understand our voices. They grew up with adoption all around them and didn't think of themselves as different; in fact, Mali used to think that being adopted was normal. Both Amalie and Joseph's adoptions were considered "open"; that is, there was a level of open communication during the adoption process. While "open" means different things in different adoptions, for ours it meant that we met the birth mothers, were in the delivery room with them, and then agreed to send annual pictures and letters to them until each child turned eighteen. These annual letters shared the joys of our journey with our chosen children and the joys of our faith in Christ.

In 2012 Mali was married and started a new adventure in her life, one she and her husband, Jason, hope will be filled with both foster children and eventually adoptive children. Shortly after their wedding, we learned that Mali's birth mother, Lois, had terminal cancer and asked to meet with us. After much prayer, wrestling, discernment, and tears, we journeyed to meet Lois again; it was a reunion that was just as emotional as the wedding that had just happened. We were able to thank her for the indescribable gift of our family, and our daughter shared the gospel of Christ with her. She shared her life story and described how her adoption had caused her to be chosen twice; once by us and once by God.

We were blessed in the process to form a relationship with Amalie's biological siblings, with whom we now have a special connection. They shared with us the significance our annual letters had been to Lois and their family. We feel that God has blessed us yet again in this process by adding more family to our lives; that's another reason He allowed this beautiful journey to happen and led us to share this incredible story.

I used to ask God why I couldn't give birth to a baby. I know that if I had the ability to write the story of my life, I wouldn't have come close to what He did. I can't imagine being a mother to any other children, and I also can't imagine missing each and every opportunity to speak of adoption and help others on their own journey. Infertility and adoption were *gifts* God gave us; He not only blessed us with the honor of being parents to our children but also gave us the gift that allowed us to find our faith in Him. Praise be to God!

Preface (Amalie)

Adoption is the way I breathe and think; it's what gets me up in the morning and warms my heart. Adoption is all I know, it's the way I think, and I wouldn't change my story for anything. But God is the sole reason I'm here today in my family and why I'm living.

While I was growing up, there was never a doubt or hesitation for me that adoption was normal. I had the privilege of growing up with adoption in every area of my life. My parents made sure I knew about the wonderful, special gift of life Lois had chosen for me. Before I could even tie my own shoes, they helped me understand that adoption was special and precious.

The concept of having a birth mom and being adopted into my family has never been difficult for me to grasp. Lois and Ruth (my brother's birth mom) have always had a special place in our family; they gave us life and then made the difficult choice to entrust our care to our adoptive parents. For this reason, I'm so grateful and honored to call myself "adopted."

Though I was very comfortable and open about my adoption, the world around me wasn't always as open. Of course, there were times when I got weird looks or heard hurtful remarks about how I was "different" or an "outcast." I tried very hard (and usually succeeded) to educate those people about what adoption was and tried to set them straight. I told them that my birth mom, Lois, loved me so much that she made a loving choice to give me the best life possible by placing me with my mom and dad. I told them that my parents chose to raise me. I was *chosen*. I *am* chosen.

Adoption, because of God, is one of the most important things in my life. When people said I was wrong, crazy, weird, or different, I took great offense, especially when people didn't take the time to understand the true love and compassion behind the decisions Lois, Ruth, and my parents had made. I felt nothing but love while growing up as a child; isn't that how you want to feel?

However, my identity isn't in being *an adopted kid*; my identity is solely in Jesus Christ. I came into this world, just like everybody else, loving parents raised me, and I'm living a full life. All this happened because God placed me inside Lois and because she placed me in the arms of my mom and dad.

When I was a child, I always pictured Lois as a woman who had a huge heart and knew exactly what she wanted. I never really pictured what she looked like—how tall she was or the color of her hair; she always seemed to be a heroine in a story from long ago. Until recently, I never thought about the reality of her life as a birth mom being difficult. After I received the first call that Lois was terminally ill, the reality hit me that she wasn't just a heroine in a story; she was a real person with real struggles.

This hero image was one of the reasons I struggled with my decision to meet Lois. I also struggled with feelings of not wanting to appear ungrateful to my parents. Then there was the fear of the unknown. I didn't want Lois's image as a heroine to be ruined. Because adoption was more natural to me than biological birth, I didn't have the "normal" identity crisis most adopted children go through. I wasn't seeking to find out who I was, where I had come from, or how to fill a void. I was content with being in my own little story. To some, this idea may give the impression that I didn't care about Lois or that she didn't matter to me, but in reality she mattered a great deal. I have tremendous respect for her and am so grateful that she chose to give me life.

CHAPTER 1

Our Infertility Journey (Karen)

But those who hope in the Lord will renew their
strength; they will soar on wings like eagles. They
will run and not grow weary. They will walk and
not be faint. —Isaiah 40:31 (NIV)

"Relax." "Take a vacation." "Take vitamins." This was the advice we received from well-meaning family and friends when we struggled to get pregnant. We longed for a baby and wished those pieces of practical advice could really help us achieve that dream. But month after month, we experienced the same disappointment—no baby. During this time, we were churchgoers and very religious, but we didn't have a personal relationship with the Lord. We knew how to face this infertility crisis with only our human determination, stubbornness, and resolve. In this crisis we prayed to God but believed we were being punished for past sins. We didn't feel God was really with us during this difficult time.

After just six months, with a known family history of infertility, we became concerned about our ability to conceive and sought a medical consultation. Initial testing confirmed our worst fears; both of us were diagnosed with infertility impairments. We opted to pursue infertility treatment and sought a reproductive endocrinologist. Having taken this step, we hoped our solution—a baby—would be close in sight. As Tom's sister Liz recalls,

> After having years of fun as a young couple, Tom and Karen decided that they were ready to have children, but after months of trying, tests were run, and the results were not what they hoped for. I vividly remember Tom asking, "Why is it that it can happen after only one time for a couple of teenagers in the backseat of a car but not for a married couple like us?"

At times during our infertility journey, Tom gave me daily hormone injections, we had scheduled intimacy, and our infertility specialist became the third person in our marriage. We had little control in this process, and as a married couple, we were rarely on the same page. Infertility tests, medical treatments, and endless disappointments took a toll on our very young marriage. When more aggressive forms of treatment were introduced, mood swings ran high for me, and Tom probably wanted to run far away. My car could drive itself to the frequent doctor's appointments, my boss could predict when I'd be gone for them, and the side effects of what was being done to my body grew increasingly challenging. Our families—my parents, in particular—were concerned about the effect infertility drugs could have on me. Liz wrote,

> Shortly after starting infertility treatment, I remember Karen asking me to be the person who would say no if their doctors should want to remove one of her ovaries due to the repercussions of aggressive treatments. I was a little hesitant to be put in that position, but I knew how important this was to them. To be honest, I was hoping I would never have to be faced with making that decision.

Friends started their families, and baby shower invitations became routine. It was difficult for me to celebrate with others what we couldn't have for ourselves. Jealousy was my enemy, and I had a hard time facing those situations. Mother's Day was equally painful. I had no hope that I would ever be a mother who someday would be able to celebrate that sacred day.

It seemed that every month started with great hope and ended with bitter disappointment. As the months moved on, our finances dwindled. We were drained emotionally and felt we had little control in bringing an end to this journey of finding life with a baby. There were so many days when I wondered whether our dream would ever become a reality.

November 3, 1990

Dear Family and Friends,

It is with great sadness that we have to tell you of the loss of our baby. The baby was almost ten weeks into its development when it was taken from us. We were privileged to have had the experience of a pregnancy but must once again pick up the pieces and go on. We have not yet decided in what way we will proceed to have our next child. It will be a difficult decision for us to make, and we ask for your prayers and thoughts to help us through this time in our lives.

Because adoption is still a strong possibility for us, we ask once again that you keep us in mind for any situations that may come about that could lead us to a baby. We would ask that you mention our situation to your area clergy as well as others that may have exposure to situations, which could create an adoptive lead for us. Also, we would like to ask that you check with your local newspapers, and inquire whether they allow advertisements for independent adoptions. Any information that you could obtain for us would be greatly appreciated.

We thank you for your support and prayers. Although this has been a difficult experience, it is comforting to know that our family and friends are there to help. Please call us collect, anytime, if you find information that could help us find an adoptive situation.

Tom and Karen

Chapter 2

Mountains and Valleys (Karen)

After facing two years of tests, drugs, and injections, and after enduring month after month of heartbreaking results, we were utterly discouraged. I clearly remember the day that changed all that. As we left town for a short vacation, we stopped at our infertility specialist's office for yet more expected negative pregnancy test results. To our astonishment, our doctor came into the room, smiling, as we finally heard the words we'd longed to hear—we were pregnant!

We were overjoyed and felt we could finally get on with our lives. We showed our first ultrasound pictures to Tom's grandfather, who wasn't expected to live much longer. We shared the news with our parents, families, and anyone who would listen. I remember the expressions on their faces, their excited voices, and their surprised reactions as we delivered the news. Relief, joy, and happiness surrounded us, and we were ready to begin living another phase of our lives.

We became stereotypical expectant parents. We dreamed of how our child would look, what sex it would be, and how much it would be loved. We planned our nursery. I bought maternity clothes. Papa (my dad) made plans to build a cradle. There was so much excitement.

But during our first trimester, at ten weeks, I had symptoms that concerned me. I went to our infertility specialist, who couldn't find a heartbeat. While he assured me this wasn't necessarily a worst-case scenario and sent me to another office with more advanced equipment, I already suspected the end result. I called Tom in distress and could barely communicate what had happened. I was in disbelief. I shut down and struggled to get through the next few days.

At our next appointment, the ultrasound technician wasn't aware of our circumstances. He was excited for us to see our baby move until he realized our situation and confirmed what we already knew. In that single moment, our dreams of the precious life we ached for were lost, and our hearts were broken. The thinly stretched seams of my life were torn apart.

As if our loss wasn't enough, I faced not only one but two medical procedures. Unfortunately, nature didn't allow my body to work without medical intervention. The first procedure was heartbreaking, especially when I was asked to sign consent for a spontaneous abortion. I was devastated. I wasn't choosing to end my baby's existence. I cried for days. I was so grateful Tom had asked my mom to come stay with us. I don't know what I would have done without her support and love as I grieved.

A few weeks later, our infertility specialist determined that the first procedure had failed, because the previous doctor hadn't completed it properly. Though our specialist normally helped couples achieve pregnancy, he wanted to put an end to this chapter for us. So he personally performed the second procedure, which allowed us to put the loss behind us, at least in theory.

We chose to name our baby Cecelia Lee. We didn't know whether it was a boy or girl, so we named it after Tom's grandmother and grandfather. For us, giving this precious life a name made our loss more tangible. While the miscarriage was significant to us, we came to realize that many around us couldn't understand the magnitude of what we experienced. There was no funeral, no obituary, and no formal closure to honor the memory of this life. We grieved, but the world around us didn't fully understand our loss. "It will get better." "You can try again." "You're young." They were all well-meaning expressions of sympathy, but they didn't fill our empty arms.

During the months and even years to follow, I kept a journal that helped me get through the difficult days. This is one of the entries.

Our precious miracle baby, ... your creation, was not that of a "normal" child's but one that was brought on by much love through scientific technology ... more than two years after we started trying to have a child, we learned of your existence. We were completely shocked, not believing that suddenly all of our prayers, hopes, and dreams were finally going to come true. Our miracle baby's life had finally begun!

At six weeks, we saw you for the first time. You were so small—just a gray blurb growing in an oval form. We couldn't see your heartbeat yet, but we knew you were there. One week later you were a little bigger—but most important was that we saw the pulsing flicker of your heartbeat.

By that time, most of our family and friends knew about you. The excitement, especially from your grandparents, was overwhelming. Everyone kept all three of us in their prayers, hoping that all would be well. Mommy felt like a normal expectant mother. Daddy was very protective of his little baby and kissed you good night every night and told you to keep growing strong and healthier.

As the days went on, our excitement and anticipation grew strong. Everything was wonderful, our precious baby, until a few weeks later. I didn't feel quite right, and went to see the doctor. To our disbelief, we were told that you stopped growing and that your heartbeat couldn't be found. We couldn't believe it! That day, we were able to see your head, your body, and the umbilical cord – how could anything be wrong? You looked like a baby – our baby – we wouldn't accept that anything wrong had happened to you. We prayed that you were okay, but somehow we knew you were not.

Our precious baby, our miracle child, our dreams for so long that came true. Suddenly into our lives, suddenly out of our lives. We thank God always for giving us the privilege of having you – of experiencing you, of being parents to you – if only for a few short weeks. Our love for you, little baby, knows no bounds. Our love for you is endless and forever.

Our hearts are broken, our arms still empty… we may never again experience life as we had with you, dear baby, so your brief existence was <u>very</u> special to us, and we shall love you forever and never forget you, our precious miracle baby.

To Us You Will Exist

To us you will exist in the flowers,
in the trees, and all things of nature
God has given us.
You are now in a world of peace and happiness
forever.
Pray for us as we pray for you, and somewhere
sometime we shall join you, our little precious
one.

-Author unknown

CHAPTER 3

The Shortest Pregnancy (Karen)

As difficult as our loss was, we were blessed to have had Liz and Craig (Tom's sister and brother-in-law) and close friends, Jay and Kim, in our lives to help us through it. I don't know how we would have journeyed through those days without them, and I am so grateful that they were there as our support system. Liz saw the mountaintops and valleys during our journey:

> I was there to witness Tom and Karen lose their precious child to miscarriage. It was painful to see their sorrow as they struggled to deal with why this had happened and where they would go from there. This is when they asked themselves if infertility treatment was really the journey they wanted to take to have a child.
>
> Instead, they decided to reach out to family and friends. They wrote a letter explaining the struggles they had faced stressing that all they really wanted was a child. So the search for a child had begun.

Tom and Karen decided that they would look into adoption as their way to grow their family. I think they knew this was the right way to go about it.

For two months we mourned the loss of our baby. Neither of us was on the same page through the grieving process. Tom was ready to move on with an adoption plan, but I couldn't get beyond the pain and emptiness I felt. After some time passed, I came to understand that a baby was what we wanted and what I longed for. So we sent letters to our family and friends, asking them to keep us in mind if an adoptive situation presented itself. We had no idea how that one letter would change the course of our lives forever.

I remember the first phone call; it came a couple of days after Christmas from Tom's cousin Pat. Her friend was expecting a baby, had already made a plan for adoption, and wanted to meet with us. I tried to process what I had heard, not allowing myself to believe that we could actually have a baby, protecting myself from another disappointment. As Pat recalls,

> I remember the day Lois called me and told me she had talked to an adoption agency and was going to place the baby. I was torn; it was like she was giving up a niece or nephew of mine.
>
> I called my mom, when I got off the phone with Lois, and told her what was going on and how upset I was. She listened for a bit and then asked, "What about Tom and Karen?" They had sent out a letter looking to adopt a child a couple weeks or so before this.
>
> Well, you could have slapped me in the head when Mom said this! I got all excited and called Lois to see if she would consider it. We cried and talked about the baby and Lois' other two children

and what would be best for the baby; of course we also talked about Tom and Karen.

So I called them and we all figured out a time they could meet Lois. They met at my house; there was no doubt in Lois's mind that she would like them to adopt her child.

Two days later, we met Lois and her children, Jenaya and Bryan (then six and eleven). We were nervous and anxious, with no expectation of what was to come. Lois started our conversation by asking whether we would be in the delivery room with her. She had already made her decision; she'd chosen us to parent her baby. We were shocked and unprepared. Being the young professionals that we were, we prepared a few pages of questions to ask; it was an interview of sorts. Lois shared information about her health history, her interests, how she planned to cope with the adoption, and what future contact she wanted. We, in turn, shared information with her so she could envision what her child's life would be like with us. While we asked many of our questions, it was so clear to us that Lois's decision wasn't based on what information we gave her, so we redirected our conversation and got to know this wonderful person.

Lois explained that she was in the process of a divorce and thought she would struggle to raise another child. We asked Bryan and Jenaya questions about things they liked. They let us know about special toys that were important to them (we kept that information close and remembered their requests at Christmas that year) and told us about some of the sports they liked and hoped the baby would enjoy.

Though Lois felt comfortable with us and asked us to make an adoption plan with her, we surprisingly told her we had to think about it. The truth is, when the gift was handed to us, we were afraid. We'd just lost a baby and were still processing that loss—and now someone from out of the blue wanted us to parent her baby? It just seemed too easy.

Lois's son, Bryan, shares what went into Lois's decision to place her baby for adoption:

Lois Stueve-Roiger was thirty-three when she found out that she was pregnant. Though she was in the process of a divorce filled with much turmoil, it never once crossed Mom's mind to abort the baby. With the stress of the divorce Mom fell into a very bad state of depression. She ultimately realized that because she was having a hard enough time caring for herself, my sister, and me she couldn't bring another child into her world at that point in time.

She started to look at her options. Mom, being the person that she was, did everything in her life for her kids. If Mom had a ripped pair of jeans and it was the only pair she owned, but one of her kids needed a new pair of shoes for school, she would get the new pair of shoes over a pair of jean for herself. It didn't matter that we may have had two other pairs of shoes in the closet; this was a common thing for her to do.

So, when she thought about adoption options, she knew, without a doubt, that it was the best decision for her baby. Jenaya and I were so important to Mom that when she learned about open adoption she talked us through her thought process about why she felt that we couldn't keep the baby. We listened and cried with her, but in the long run we always felt that she knew best. Mom was set on an open adoption because it was a way to keep the lines of communication open in case the baby may want to meet her down the road. Most importantly open adoption was a way for her to be reassured that the adoptive parents were who Mom had expected;

better parents than what she felt she could be at that point in time.

Mom met a couple (Tom and Karen) through a mutual friend and knew right away that they were the ones that would be able to do an amazing job with her baby. Jenaya and I got to meet them and were so excited that they wanted to talk to us! We got to answer their questions and even got to pick out what we thought should be some of the baby's first gifts (Legos and a Barbie), which were our favorite toys at the time!

On the way home, we talked about the pros and cons of adopting this baby. During that ride, Tom reminds me, God placed on his heart that this was the child He had chosen for us. We called Lois when we arrived home and moved ahead with our adoption plan. We were about to become parents, and yet disbelief kept telling me that another loss was inevitable, and I couldn't completely give in to the excitement. Since Lois was due any day, life took quite a turn.

Our family was both thrilled and guarded. Both sides of the family had adopted family members, so accepting an adopted child into the family wasn't an obstacle. But everyone had concerns—some verbalized and some not.

Fortunately, my siblings and I knew about adoption because we have seven adopted cousins; they were true blood cousins in our eyes. It didn't matter that they were adopted; we never saw them as being different.

With the adoption came many thoughts: Would the baby be born normal? What would the baby look like? Would the baby fit into our family?

Over the years, our family had witnessed family members have "unexpected" pregnancies.

Some opted to keep their child while others decided to place their child for adoption. This was also a process that my family and I were familiar with so we were ready to embrace the process of an adopted child.

I knew Lois as the friend of my cousin, Pat. She was a selfless woman who would be gifting her child to Tom and Karen so they could become the parents of her biological baby. Little did she know that she was not gifting her child to just them but to an entire family who would love that child unconditionally and eagerly!   -Liz

The next sixteen days were the shortest pregnancy we could have known. After our miscarriage, we'd torn down the drywall in the room that would have been the nursery, so we had no room, no furniture—nothing was prepared for a baby. We shopped for all the baby basics and had many inquisitive people wondering whom these things were for since I was clearly not pregnant. We enlisted the help of an adoption agency to rush through our home study and all the necessary legal paperwork for us to become adoptive parents and be able to bring the baby home from the hospital; this was a process that typically took months.

Those sixteen days were some of the most exciting ones we had. Our friend Kim recalls one day in particular:

We got the call from Karen saying they had two weeks to prepare for a baby and needed my help. Jay and I had a daughter, not quite two years old at the time. So off Karen and I went to shop on a Sunday afternoon to get ready for the coming baby. We practically bought out the baby department; we had so much fun!

Two full carts later at the checkout-counter, the clerk looked at both of us strangely, but did not say a word. Neither of us was pregnant! Karen then spoke up and told her that they were adopting and the awkward silence turned into laughter. This is a memory that Karen and I will cherish forever!

Because cell phones didn't yet exist, we relied solely on our home phone for baby updates from our cousin Pat. When our phone line went down for three days, we temporarily moved in with Liz and Craig so as not to miss *the* call to go to the hospital. When the call finally came, the experience was like being in a slow-motion movie. The car ride was surreal, and everything about that day, January 14, 1991, seemed like a dream …

Lois was wonderful. With her sister supporting her, she allowed us to be involved in as much of the experience as we could. When Lois walked the halls to induce labor, Tom had a wheelchair in tow, concerned that she was going to drop at any time. Lois and I had some good talks and some great laughs at Tom's reactions; and while we were almost strangers to each other, she made sure we experienced everything we could and helped us feel very comfortable.

When the time came for her delivery, Lois was firm in her resolve that we were to witness the birth. Looking back, I think she needed to see our reaction to this baby to make sure she was making the right choice. With tears, excitement, and so much love, we saw our firstborn child arrive into the world and heard her first cries. I was so blessed to be the first person to hold her. We were in love with each other and with this precious daughter God had literally dropped from heaven into our empty arms.

Brian and Jenaya share what they remember:

January 14th came quickly and there was a new baby girl. Mom found out that the new baby was going to be named Amalie, but through the course of the last couple of months, she told my sister and me that we could also name her so that she will always be a part of our family even if she is not here right now. So Amalie was named Krista, in our family, and that is who she was to us until the day we met her again years later.   -Bryan

I honestly don't recall my mom being pregnant. I was six years old when she met Tom and Karen and had turned seven only four days before Amalie was born. I recall going to the hospital and also meeting Tom and Karen, but those memories are vague.   -Jenaya

We named her Amalie Elizabeth after two great-grandmothers; her first name fulfilled a longtime dream I had of naming a daughter after my beloved grandmother before she died; in fact, it was just a few short weeks later that she, at age ninety-four, met her namesake. We chose her middle name in honor of Tom's grandmother.

At the time of Mali's birth, it was uncommon for adoptive parents to be in the delivery room. The hospital staff went above and beyond with the unique set of circumstances and helped to make it a very joyous experience for us. They allowed us to participate in every aspect of the labor and delivery, and they gave us special time in the "staff only" nursery to spend with our new little baby and bond with her. Their care and concern for Lois and us were more than we could have asked for. We believe the experience was what Lois wanted and what allowed me, in particular, to deal with some of the grief I was still working out from our miscarriage.

A strong bond developed between Lois and us that day. I can't begin to describe the emotional attachment we made with her. Having the privilege of being chosen to parent this perfect baby and then being blessed to see her be born into this world were beyond anything we could have imagined. She'd chosen us to be Amalie's parents; that was amazing. But we soon realized that her choice to allow us to be parents meant that there would be a loss for her. As we left the hospital that night, we began to clearly understand that.

We made many celebratory phone calls that night announcing our miracle baby to her grandparents, aunts, and uncles. The tears, excitement, and love we heard warmed our hearts. There was our shopping trip, minutes before closing hours, to find a "coming home" outfit for the next day; it was two sizes too big for her, but it was all we could find before the store closed.

We had so much fun, so much happiness, and yet despite all the excitement, there was still an air of caution. Would Lois change her mind that night? Was she holding Amalie, bonding with her? Did her children and family see Amalie? Did they beg her to change her mind? We could understand if they did; she was so beautiful. We tried to put these ideas out of our minds, but they stayed with us until the next morning.

When we returned to the hospital, we were able to continue to get to know our little daughter. Lois had requested that we bring Amalie home from the hospital with us. Our social worker reminded us that we were taking a legal risk, as Lois would have a few weeks, during which time she could change her mind and take the baby back. We were resolved to take her home with us and hoped and prayed she would be ours forever.

We brought roses to Lois that day to express the love and appreciation we had for her and for the decision that changed our lives. She presented a baby blanket to us, which members of a local church had made; what a precious keepsake for Amalie! In our final moments together, we made a promise to Lois to write annual letters to her until Amalie's eighteenth birthday. After that time, it would be Amalie's decision whether to pursue contact.

Lois, being the beautiful person she was, hugged us both and told us to take Amalie home and be her parents. She left that room and placed that precious life in our care. I remember feeling conflicted. On the one hand, I was so happy to finally be a mom; on the other hand, I felt a burden for the pain Lois must have been going through at that moment and would likely feel in the days to come.

We found the next few weeks to be some of the most joy-filled and challenging of our lives. We had finally achieved the fulfillment of our dream of having a child, and I grew more in love with this precious baby girl every moment. And yet I struggled with so many questions. Will Lois come back for her? Will she change her mind? Surely if she saw this baby again, she would be convinced that she hadn't made the right decision.

My conflicting thoughts came from an inner struggle I didn't understand, one that would come into focus as time went on. This was the most beautiful baby in the world; would I have been brave enough to do what Lois had done? Over the years, Tom and I have asked that question of ourselves about both of our children. Would we truly have been able to do what both Lois and Ruth did? Would we have been able to entrust these precious gifts to fill someone else's empty arms?

God chose two women who were brave and strong beyond what we could comprehend; to our realization, they were beyond what we could probably have done ourselves. Though we sat on pins and needles during those next few "legal risk" weeks, Lois didn't change her mind, and Amalie's adoption became final, and we became her forever parents. When the final court date took place a few months later and the judge declared her to be our adopted child, the event was only a formality of what had already taken place in our hearts. This was the child God had chosen for us to parent through a very special set of circumstances, and we were very blessed.

Infertility was a struggle for both of us, but I later concluded that if I could have written the script of my life, I wouldn't have changed one thing God chose for us. If I could do it all over again, I would go through every month of pain and disappointment, every tear, and even the miscarriage to have the outcome of what we were blessed to receive.

Jenaya recently shared that she and her husband also struggled with infertility. We came from two different worlds but arrived at a similar conclusion.

> I agree 100% it's God's plan. After Jesse and I struggled with infertility and then got pregnant and with so many things happening after that, I started to believe more that God has a reason for His plan for us. We may not understand it when the plan goes in a direction we don't prefer (like Mom getting cancer), but I TRULY believe that His plan was to lead us to your family. And, to be honest, if I didn't think this way, I would not be able to get through Mom's death. It's been hard, as you know, but every day I wake up and I look at Mom's picture and know she is watching over me and my family like she always did. It helps comfort my heart.

Dear Birthmother,

We are a family of three, blessed with our daughter, Amalie (Mali for short), through the miracle of adoption. We are now anxious to expand our family with another infant.

Following college and our marriage in 1986 we (Tom, twenty-nine and Karen, twenty-eight) bought a home in a friendly suburban Minneapolis neighborhood, where we are all active members in our churches; Tom as a member of a Catholic parish where he has, in the past, been active in his choir and Karen and Mali as members of a Lutheran parish where Karen is involved with Christian education and Mali is enrolled in Sunday School and the children's choir.

As a family, we enjoy doing many things together – we especially love the outdoors and traveling. We have completed three courses of swimming lessons for Mali, who has become our little fish! During the summer we enjoy walks to the park with our dog, Einstein, and going to the beach in warm weather. In the past, we have enjoyed vacationing in Florida and visiting relatives who live out of state.

After a few years of unsuccessful medical treatment and a miscarriage, we chose to create our family through adoption. Just two weeks before her birth, we learned of Mali's birth mother. We were able to meet her and her two children to discuss each other's wishes for Mali's future. We were privileged to have seen Mali born into our lives and have cherished every day we have had with her.

Mali is an energetic and happy little two year old who has changed our lives more than we ever thought possible. She has allowed us to relive our childhoods as we now see the world through her eyes. Our love for her could be no greater for she is more than our adopted child – she is our chosen child.

We are now seeking a second child as we have found parenting to be a rewarding experience and feel we are ready to share our love and lives with another child. Our extended family has been supportive of our adoption plans and is anxiously awaiting the arrival of a new addition as well.

We would appreciate the opportunity to talk with you about your dreams for your child.

Tom, Karen and Mali

Chapter 4

Filling a Void (Karen)

I wish I could say that after Mali and Joe were born, the pain of our miscarriage went away; but it didn't. It took a long time for me to heal, though the pain decreased as our joy increased with the miracle of each new day with Mali and later with Joe. I found that I loved and longed for the baby we'd lost but that God had sent us our miracle babies to fill our hearts. I couldn't imagine not having Mali and Joe, and while I wished I could hold Cecelia, we had the babies we were meant to have on this side of heaven.

Around the time of Cecelia's due date, Tom gave me a card I held onto all of these years.

> Some people
> > Come into our lives
> > and quickly go.
> Some stay for awhile
> > leave footprints
> > on our hearts
> > and we are never,
> > ever the same.

> > > -Flavia

Honey:

This was supposed to be the happiest day of our lives since the day we were married. Instead we are left with the wonderful feelings of what Cecelia Lee's conception brought to our lives. Although the baby was with us only a short time, he/she left us never to be the same again. Cecelia Lee reminded us that life is fragile and sacred and prepared us to fully appreciate the arrival of our beautiful little girl!

There is a purpose behind all that has happened in our lives over the past couple of years and I believe that we were being prepared to become the best parents possible to Amalie. Although we've weathered stormy times, I'd do it all again to be her father!

I love you!

Tom

In 1992, when Mali was a year and a half old, we decided it was time for a second child. While we briefly considered infertility treatment and went in for a consult, we concluded that biology was no longer important to us. Mali was ours, and we couldn't imagine life without her. While I dreamed of being pregnant again, the dream was to carry a baby, not to have one that was biologically tied to us, so we went back to networking with hope that our second baby would arrive soon.

Our networking was extensive. We researched different ways to advertise that would reach a younger population. Most advertising was done in college-town papers.

> ADOPTION: Young college grads and toddler daughter wish to adopt baby. Loving, family-oriented, Christian, energetic. Call collect (Tom/Karen). Adoption – a loving choice.

We also sent out hundreds of letters to family, friends, churches, doctors' offices, high school counselors, and so forth. We gave suggestions to our network of family and closest friends as to how they could network for us. We tried to use every creative and "out of the box" outreach we could think of to spread our message.

Because of our networking letters, we were soon connected with a fifteen-year-old birth mother through a close family friend. We traveled to Florida to meet with her and her boyfriend, who chose us to parent their baby. We made an adoption plan, worked with an adoption agency, talked with her regularly, and counted down the days until this new baby would join our family. Toward the end of the pregnancy and just prior to the birth at Christmastime, the birth mother decided to keep her baby. While we were grieved, we both came to accept that the situation wasn't meant to be, so we held on to the hope that there was another baby for us—and there was!

A few weeks later, a family member contacted my mom, Lillian, to share information about a couple from their church looking for an adoptive family. As she recalls:

> I talked with my cousin and mentioned that Tom and Karen were looking for another baby. Somehow the word got passed on to another cousin who knew of friends that were going to place a baby for adoption.

The couple was married with a three-year-old daughter and had other children who had been previously placed for adoption. They couldn't financially afford another child and had been working with an adoption agency, but they were unhappy with the choices of adoptive parents they had been given. They were interested in meeting with us, so our next journey began.

We first met Ruth and Wes at a restaurant, once again excited, nervous, anxious, and filled with questions. Our conversation went back and forth, giving them the comfort level they needed to choose us to be the parents of their baby. Once again God took an impossible set of circumstances and began to mold them into a beautiful story. Another whirlwind pregnancy journey began, though this time we had several more weeks to prepare than we had with Mali. In a short period of time, we had several visits with Ruth, Wes, and their daughter. There were ongoing phone conversations with them and another rushed home study and adoption process with two agencies (theirs in Illinois and ours in Minnesota) that helped to fulfill the necessary interstate requirements for our new baby's arrival. We even squeezed in a short trip just the two of us (the first time we left Mali with her grandparents for that long) before the reality of two children came to be.

Since this was Ruth's fifth pregnancy, we assumed she would deliver near her due date. But just like with Lois, God allowed us extra time to get everything ready for this blessing. The long car ride to Illinois was very exciting, especially preparing Mali to become a big sister. With Mali delivered into her grandparents' care, we focused on helping Ruth get through what we knew would be an emotional experience for her.

Our second birth experience was filled with many challenges. The hospital staff wasn't as thoughtful of either Ruth's needs or the amazing adoption plan that unfolded. At times Ruth (who had public assistance for insurance) was placed in a hallway or a very small closet-sized room that meant standing room only for us. We did our best to help her through her labor, as she didn't have anyone else with her that day. Though initially she wanted only me in the delivery room, she changed her mind at the last minute and asked Tom in as well; fortunately the hospital was gracious enough to allow us both to be present.

On June 16, 1993, we were again blessed to see our precious child born into our lives. We were once again gifted with the excitement of seeing our son's birth, hearing his first cries, and holding him for the first time. How fortunate we were to have been given a second "once in a lifetime" experience to see the miracle of our son being born, even though I was unable to give birth. We were so happy that our baby was healthy and admittedly very excited that we now had a son!

Joseph Thomas, named after a cousin and Tom, was born into our world, and we were on a mountaintop. Mali was introduced to her baby brother the next day at the hospital and was ready to take on the role of the proud and protective big sister (though at times she thought she was his mother). We were twice blessed and felt our family was now complete, our infertility journey finished.

While the hospital staff wasn't very welcoming toward us when we came to visit Joe each day, we tried to make the best of the situation. In addition to the staff challenges, there were also times during the next few days when we truly thought Ruth and Wes would change their minds and decide to keep the baby. The social worker prepared us for that possibility. Our hearts longed to take Joseph home, but we knew that decision wasn't ours to make.

Ultimately, Ruth and Wes came to the conclusion that they couldn't raise another child. We believe Ruth had also wanted to see our response to this little life to make sure she was making the right choice.

We dressed our son in his homecoming outfit and said our tearful good-byes. We again made the promise to write annual letters to Ruth and Wes until Joe's eighteenth birthday. It was important to us for our contact to mirror Mali's adoption plan so that the level of our communication with Lois, Ruth, and Wes for both children was equal so neither child would feel different from the other.

Prior to Joe's leaving the hospital, I remember going to an administrative office to pick up his hospital baby photos. An older employee lamented about how sad it was that our baby's mother, Ruth, had "given up" her baby. I gently explained to her how excited we were to have the joy of adopting him. Her reaction clearly showed me that many people don't truly understand the full scope of the adoption process.

Because Joe was born in Illinois, we had interstate adoption laws that had to be fulfilled prior to returning home to Minnesota. Since the hospital was very close to my parents' home, we were able to stay with them during another "legal risk" period of time. The day after we brought Joe home from the hospital, we received a phone call from Ruth and Wes; they wanted to meet with us the next day, on Father's Day. Church that morning was strained. So many people congratulated us and expressed their excitement about our new addition, but I couldn't bond with my little Joey that day. I was so sure that he would be taken from us that afternoon. I was afraid that my heart would be broken again.

We later met Ruth, Wes, and a couple of Wes's older children at a restaurant. We were relieved that they had only wanted to see him one more time and wish us well. The following day, they signed the legal paperwork that allowed us to work toward finalizing our adoption. For the next three weeks, we adjusted to life with two children and waited for the legal issues to be cleared, allowing us to go back home. My parents were a great help, especially during the days when Tom had to go back home to Minnesota to work (though adoption costs are high, the outcome is priceless). I particularly loved the late-night walks my dad and I took trying to get Joe to go back to sleep. We had him trained to sleep through the night before our return back home.

> We were excited that we had a granddaughter and a grandson! It brought us so much joy and happiness that we could be part of the first few weeks' of Joe's life. As we didn't want Joe to get all the attention, we made sure that we did special things with Mali, too! Papa loved rocking Joe on our swing to get him to sleep...   - Lillian (Nana)

When we were finally able to return home, Tom was waiting for us with great excitement. My mother-in-law recently reminded me that Tom had made an enormous banner, which he hung on the front of our home, welcoming a son, brother, and grandson. There was much excitement and love in welcoming him home to his new family. We were ready to start the next phase of our journey as a larger family.

January 5, 1992

Dear Lois:

It's so hard to believe that a year has already passed since Amalie's birth. We hope this finds you well!

As you can see from these pictures, we've had a full year of happiness! Mali continues to be an overachiever — she began crawling at six months, walking with help at six-and-a-half months, and walking alone at eleven months. She has four teeth and continues to be a very happy and enthusiastic little girl.

She continues to amaze us all the time. She plays with objects, takes them apart and puts them back together again. She has a vocabulary of several words and talks to us constantly! She's had two small bouts with a cold/virus. She's very healthy at nineteen lbs. She's quite petite, which has stretched her wardrobe out nicely!

We took her to the YMCA for swimming lessons at six months old — she loves the water. She "tested" her skills in the ocean on our vacation in Florida last fall.

Christmas was the best we've ever had. Daddy bought her a red velvet dress — as you can see, she looked like an angel. I think we were more excited with her new toys than she was!

We hope 1992 will bring peace and happiness to you. Thank you again for bringing this miracle to us!

God's blessings —

Tom, Karen and Amalie

CHAPTER 5

The Significance of the Dear Lois Letters (Karen)

We made a commitment to both Lois and Ruth after our children were born. We promised to write letters to them each year; around the time of the children's birthdays, we sent along letters with photos that chronicled the past year. These letters would be written until each child turned eighteen. At that time it would be up to Mali and Joe as to whether they wanted to pursue communication with their birth family.

These annual letters were an emotional experience for me. I admit that there were times when I wrote them feeling sad that I hadn't given birth to my kids, and wished I could be an "ordinary mom." But those feelings dissipated as I sat down and wrote them; in fact, most years I ended up in tears, trying to imagine Lois's and Ruth's situation and their wanting to know as many details as possible to ensure that our children were doing well. I cried because these women were so brave to make a decision I don't think I would have been capable of making. I cried because I wanted to share as much as I could with them so they could feel like they were still a part of Mali and Joe's lives. I cried because my heart was overflowing with gratitude.

The letters became a way for me to pour my heart out to these wonderful women who had helped to create our family. Tom would always help me step back and tell a story with different details than I remembered or tell me to add or delete certain things I did or didn't see. We tried to paint a picture for them through words and photographs to give them peace that Mali and Joe were thriving and doing well. Throughout the years, the bond we felt with Lois and Ruth continued to be as strong as the days when they'd entrusted us with the lives of our children. We took the gift of parenting and the promise to write these letters very much to heart.

In 2012, when we reunited with Lois and her children, we found out how important these letters had been to their family. They had all the letters and pictures in a photo album; we quickly understood that these letters were an important part of Lois's adoption journey.

What I recall is that every year around my birthday we would get a letter from Amalie's parents. The letters explained what she had been up to and the pictures showed how she had grown. I don't recall my mom ever having to sit me down later to explain the adoption to me or who Amalie was. I just recall reading the letters as if I knew what was going on (I was eight when the first letter arrived).

Then, as I got into my teenage years, I remember looking forward to the day that letter arrived - always getting the mail and paging through to see if the yellow package had come. If it was later in the month we started to get nervous it wasn't going to come.

The letters were something we all looked forward to because it was a time we all sat down together, as a family, to see how our sister had grown and what accomplishments she had made. I remember being in awe when I found out that she was playing piano and that she traveled to Walt Disney World. I remember thinking there was no way she would have ever been able to experience those things had she not been adopted.

I remember when Joe was adopted thinking that they looked alike! I remember being excited that Amalie had a sibling and hoped their relationship was a lot like Bryan's and mine.

After we moved out of the house Mom would read the letters herself and then we would read them with her again when we visited her.   –Jenaya

When Bryan recalls the special letters, he remembers the transition Lois experienced following Amalie's (Krista's) adoption.

After her birth, we were told that we would be able to see Krista grow-up as we would get pictures every year so we could see how things were going; it was a way for Mom to know that Krista was being cared for.

Even though Mom knew that a letter was coming that first year, she had a very hard and anxious year of not having the baby. Many nights she would stay awake crying and I would sit with her, hug her and tell her that she was the best mom in the world and I would make things better for her someday. We would talk about Krista and Mom would tell me how nervous she was and that she had hoped she did the right thing. Because of so many things that happened in her life, trust was a hard thing for her. Mom lived for Jenaya, me and now Krista.

Krista's first birthday came and went and all I could see was pain on Mom's face. I think she felt that she did something wrong or was afraid that the letters wouldn't really come; maybe she thought they were just an empty promise. Everything was put to rest when a yellow envelope arrived in the mail around the 22nd of January. It was the first time, in a couple of years that I saw a real smile come from Mom. She opened the envelope with shaking hands and tears at the same time.

We ran to the couch and sat next to her as she read the letter out loud to us. As soon as the letter was done we looked at the pictures. We commented on things we saw and the cool Christmas tree they had. Of course, Mom, being the person she was, wanted us to be happy; she pointed out that we helped pick out Krista's Christmas gifts and pointed to the pictures with the Lego's box and the Barbie.

She was so happy, full of relief, and excited to show anyone and everyone the amazing letter that came with pictures of her baby girl, which showed how well Krista was being taken care of. She would brag, in a sense, about how happy she was with the choice of Krista's parents and that she knew that she had done the right thing. Our sitting on the couch became a very common thing in our house around the 22nd of every January.

A few years down the road we got a letter and pictures of Krista's new addition to her family; her baby brother, Joe. We were all super excited; Jenaya and I thought it was so cool because now she had a brother like I had a sister and vice versa.

We didn't get the luxury of having her by us as she grew up but we did have the luxury of not just growing up watching our sister become a wonderful woman that she is today but also watching a brother of hers growing up to become an outstanding young man that he is today. Many tears, many laughs, and many happy comments were made over the course of eighteen years.

Even when my sister and I moved out of the house we always knew that Mom wanted us home or at least close to our phones around the 22nd of January. We did just that for her over and over again, because our family wasn't complete without knowing what Krista and Joe did over the course of the year.

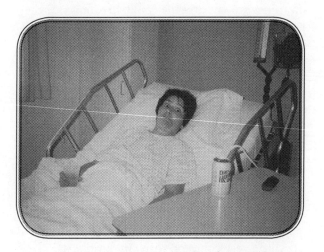

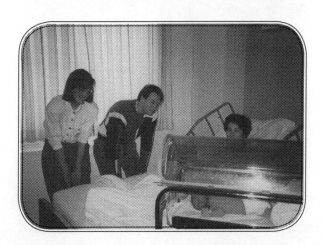

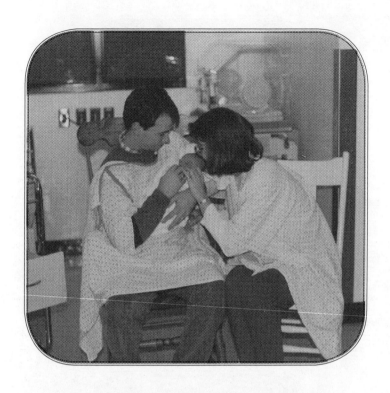

December 29, 1992

Dear Lois,

We hope that you had a wonderful Christmas and holiday season. It's hard to believe that another year has already passed. This year has been full of a lot of changes.

It's hard to know where to begin. We've seen Mali change from a baby into a sweet little girl this year. She has a very spirited personality; always smiling and laughing. She's starting to talk sentences and tries to carry on conversations. She's full of questions and even full of answers! She's a fast learner and amazes us at things she says and does.

We started potty training this summer. Though we're not quite there yet, she's done real well. Just before Christmas we took down her crib and she now enjoys her "big girl" bed.

This fall we went to Disney World where Mali got to sit on Mickey's lap and visit the other Disney characters. She just finished her third set of swimming lessons and has turned into quite a fish. She'll even jump to us without any help!

Every Sunday, Mali asks when we are going to church. She can't wait to get there! She was in her first Christmas program in December. While the older kids sang, Mali livened up things by dancing on the stage!

Christmas was a lot of fun this year. Mali had great fun opening up everyone's gifts! She had a nice visit with Santa, too.

We had hoped to tell you that we were getting another baby in January. As you've probably heard, that didn't work out. We worked with a teenage birth mother for five months and were disappointed when she decided to parent the baby. We are praying that God will bless us with another baby in 1993. If you hear of any situations, please pass them along – we're getting ready for an all-out search in January.

It seems that every day with Amalie becomes more and more precious to us. We want to thank you again for allowing us the privilege to be parents to this beautiful little girl. We hope and pray that you and your family are well.

Love,

Tom, Karen & Amalie

December 31, 1993

Dear Lois:

We hope this holiday season finds you well! It's hard to believe that yet another year has passed again! What a year it was…

This year was a year of firsts and of changes. Since turning two, Mali has learned all sorts of new things. She has known the alphabet and has been counting to ten since shortly after her birthday. She talks complete sentences…my dad feels (and we all agree) that she is a gifted little girl. She's far advanced for most kids her age. She always wants to learn more!

Of course, the biggest change was the addition of our little Joseph Thomas. Just as with Mali's birth, we were again blessed to see our little Joey born into the world. Since he was born in Chicago, I and the kids stayed with my folks for 2 ½ weeks before we could come home. Mali saw her brother in the hospital the day after he was born. As you can see, she is a proud big sister. She is a wonderful helper and is very protective of Joey.

Instead of regressing in her habits, as many people said she could, Mali progressed after Joey came. She became potty trained in July and was rewarded with her first tricycle. She has also given up her pacifier, as she says "they're for babies!"

Mali now has a swing set in our back yard, which is her favorite activity in the summer. She loves the snow, too, and likes to sled and make snow angels.

She was a star in her Sunday School program this year, and even though she ran down the aisle to find Daddy halfway through, she did sing a couple of songs— another favorite pastime of hers!

We went to see Ringling Brothers' Circus this year—we think she may have been a bit young yet as she sat and stared during the whole performance, with no reaction!! But she had quite a lot to say for weeks after!

Finally, as you can see, Mali made her debut as a flower girl for her aunt. What a beautiful one she was. She'll get to repeat her performance this fall for her uncle's wedding!

That takes us to date, I think! Lois, we again express our thanks to you for this miracle!

God's blessings to you in 1994!

Love,

Tom and Karen

December 26, 1994

Dear Lois:

We hope you and your family had a wonderful holiday! Once again it's hard to believe that another year has passed! '94 was a year of a lot of change for us!

The biggest change in Mali this year is the transition from a toddler into a little girl. She is a petite, 34 lb. almost four-year-old with a bubbly personality; she keeps us on our toes! She talks complete sentences and grows smarter by the day! She is very creative and loves to paint, draw, color, etc. She constantly asks questions about everything she can think of!

After the death of my grandmother (Mali's namesake) in April, we made the biggest change of the year and relocated to Wisconsin. I had a relocation opportunity with my company and we felt that being closer to the grandparents was a great thing to do. Tom found a job within a few weeks after we moved and although we had to live in a small apartment for two months, we moved into our dream house in June. We now have four bedrooms and a large yard in a new neighborhood. We found a new church where Mali goes to Sunday School and found a daycare very close to home.

Both the kids are adapting well with the new daycare after leaving the sitter in Minneapolis whom they both had since birth. In fact, Mali has been doing so well that they moved her into the four-year-old pre-school room in September as they felt she was ready for the challenge. She adores her teacher (and vice versa) and is now learning to write her ABC's and name, art and science projects, etc.! She's even learned our phone number and how to call 9-1-1! She's made a lot of new friends and loves being a "school kid"!

Before moving, Mali was diagnosed with reflux of her kidneys. Essentially she had a kidney infection that continued to re-infect the kidney without getting the infection out. Her other kidney was felt to be underdeveloped. Fortunately, after months of tests and medication, the infection is gone and the smaller kidney grew to normal size. We continue to give her daily medication, but she should be fine.

She completed one course of swimming lessons and will have more this winter; then on to ballet lessons... she calls herself a ballerina and wears the tutu that came from Santa all day long; those should be fun lessons!

As Pat probably told you, she had a repeat performance as a flower girl in her uncle's wedding in October. She did great!

Santa visited Mali and Joey on Christmas Eve at home. She thought that was great. And, of course, there are brotherly and sisterly battles going on as to who can play with whose new toys!

What can we say? Mali's a sweet loving little girl. She's a wonderful sister to her little brother whom she adores and she's a daughter who grows dearer to us each day.

Thank you for this miracle. We wish you and your family the best in 1995.

Love,

Tom and Karen

December 27, 1995

Dear Lois,

We hope this letter finds all of you doing well. We had a wonderful Christmas — it's hard to believe that another year has passed again!

Well, where do we begin? Mali is in preschool at her daycare and is doing very well! She can spell and write her name, can say her phone number/address and is starting to spell words. Pretty soon Tom and I are going to have to stop spelling things we don't want the kids to know about! We've started the search for schools for next year and are between a Christian school and a very strong public school close to our home. It's amazing to us that in just a few months she'll be school bound! Where does time go?!

The big "news" for us is that we joined a very active non-denominational church this summer and are now able to worship together as a family. Mali and Joey are both going to Sunday School and we plan to be very active as a family in this church—the Lord has blessed us to have found it! Mali comes home after Sunday School excited to talk about Jesus or whatever Bible story she learns about — it's great to see!

This year, we have been blessed to have had two new additions added to our family — Mali and Joey finally have cousins and Mali is very proud to take on her role as Sr. cousin (as you can see in the picture with her cousin, Lauren!). She already has plans to be the mother, teacher, etc.!

We had wonderful news this summer —Mali outgrew the kidney problems we wrote to you about last year. The infections are gone and both kidneys are the *same size. We have to have periodic tests to monitor, but they expect no more problems!!*

Mali has been very active this year. Between ballet, swimming and gymnastics lessons, it seems like we are on the run constantly! She'll start gymnastics again after the new year (she can do summersaults, cartwheels, can flip on the bars, and walk pretty gracefully on the beam!) and can't wait!

After spending a few weekends with my folks and a week with Tom's Mom and sister, we all packed up for a vacation to Door County, WI and to the Dells. Mali especially enjoyed the beach and going to the petting farm. At the Dells we went to a water park and were there all day long!! We had a great time! Fortunately, our move has been great as we seem to see our folks a lot more, which is nice!

Mali and Joey are going through sibling rivalry, but Mali is very protective of Joe at school – he is going through speech therapy and she makes it a point to ask the therapist what she is doing. She's quite a little mother at home!

Her birthday (fourth) started with her first kid's party at McDonald's. This next birthday will be on the thirteenth at the YMCA. She'll have about ten to twelve of her friends for games, fun and action in the Kid's Gym.

As always, Lois, we thank you for this miracle—we cherish her every day of our lives. We thank God that you came into our lives and pray always for your peace and happiness.

All the best in 1996—With our love,

Tom, Karen, Mali and Joey

January 1, 1997

Dear Lois:

Here we are again – another year – it's amazing how quickly time has passed! This past year, especially, has been packed for us!

Let's see…Mali is finally growing! She's 43" tall and weighs 42 lbs. She's extremely active (loves gymnastics classes) and very smart (we bought a computer this year and her first question was whether or not it had a CD Rom)! As you can see in more recent photos, she's got shorter hair now. She's much happier to not deal with the tangles (patience is not a virtue of hers!)

The beginning part of the year was really non-eventful for us. This summer, after fighting several ear infections, Mali had tubes put in both ears. She was a brave little girl and shed not one tear. She's been doing much better since then.

In June, she lost the first of three bottom teeth. She loved the tooth fairy and is looking forward to her front teeth coming out soon! She started to ride a two-wheeler with training wheels this year and Daddy is determined to wean her off those this year.

The first day of school and since has been the pinnacle of the year for her. She clung on to my leg until her new teacher pried her off me and took her away to a new phase in her life! Of course, I cried for hours until I saw her smiling face later that day. That smile continues everyday as she really likes school a lot! Our first conferences went very well and her teachers tell us that she is conscientious, considerate and a quick learner.

She especially likes computer class (but art, music, gym, and library are close in line) and participates in all areas. She's made many new friends, too! I spent a morning with her class at the zoo before Christmas—we had a lot of fun.

As always we've spent a lot of time with our extended families. We had a reunion with Tom's side this summer. Mali and Joey stayed with my folks for a week this fall while Tom and I went to Cancun for our ten-year anniversary. Because of normal sibling rivalry, I think my folks were glad to see us back!

We have all been very involved with our church. I started an infertility and adoption support ministry and Tom began a men's ministry Bible study group. Mali and Joey continue to be involved in Sunday School and Mali is in a large (100+ voice) choir at church for Kindergartners and first graders!

Mali has really grown up this year. She's a happy, energetic, bubbly little – or I'd better say – big girl who has a heart of gold. She lights up any room she walks in—it seems that everyone adores her!

Well, until next year we hope and pray that you and your family are healthy and happy and that God will bless all of you in 1997.

Love,

Tom and Karen

January 2, 1998

Dear Lois,

Happy 1998! We hope and pray that you will have a blessed New Year. If '98 is anything like '97 was, we'll have a great one!

I know we say it every year, but this one was another year of firsts!

We were fortunate to have done a lot of traveling this year. Mali and I took an Amtrak ride (her first) to visit some close friends in Missouri. They have an eight year old who Mali has grown up with; she and Megan had a ball!

We then went to the Wisconsin Dells in August with Tom's sister and family. The weather wasn't the best, but we had fun. Mali's new activity is now go-carting! We then went to Sanibel Island, Florida, in October w/Tom's Mom. The kids had a great time at the beach; they were especially happy to spend a week with Grandma!

As you can see, Mali got a new bike last birthday. She was very apprehensive about riding it until about July. After that we never saw her as she was always on a bike ride!

First grade has been great! Good reports come from her teacher and reading is coming along very well! She apparently has become the popular one as she's invited fifteen of her friends to her upcoming birthday party!

She couldn't get her baby teeth (front) out, so the dentist had to pull them and then after they finally grew in, she had a little spill and cracked one of them! We're waiting for it to grown back – then she'll likely get a crown.

She's also joined Brownies and has also continued with gymnastics. We think she's found her passion so we're going to let her keep on tumbling! Mali continues to enjoy her Sunday School class. The first graders get to sing periodically to older kids and in church. She loves to sing songs about Jesus!

The biggest change in our lives is that Tom has bought into a screen-printing business and is now self-employed. Our hope is that I can work part-time and be home with the kids more.

It's amazing how quickly Mali is turning into a little lady! Just before Christmas vacation, Mali's class had a gift exchange. She got a pair of pierced earrings – since she doesn't have pierced ears, this posed a problem. Her teacher sent a nice note home that day saying, "I have to compliment you on the wonderful job you are doing teaching Mali to be a kind and thoughtful person. She got a pair of earrings in the gift exchange but managed to hide her disappointment and graciously thanked the giver..." Needless to say, this was a tearjerker and she couldn't understand why I was crying! I've since shared this note with all who enter our home!

God bless you, Lois! We pray that you are healthy and happy and that you have a blessed 1998!

Love,

Tom and Karen

December 30, 1998

Dear Lois:

It seems like every year we say the same thing — yet another year of huge changes. It's been one of those years — again!!! We hope this finds you in good health and we hope you had a blessed Christmas!

Following a recent growth spurt, 58 lbs. Mali is full of a lot of energy and spunk! She loves life and tries to do as much as she can to enjoy it. The best way to describe her is a light that shows her love of God to all those she comes in contact with.

We started off '98 with a rather large birthday party with about fifteen of her friends (yes, she is still the social butterfly!) painting t-shirts! Since Tom is an owner of a screen printing company, t-shirts have become a way of life and painting them seemed like a great idea. The girls had fun.…the adults were worn out!

Mali continues to be in Brownies and Pioneer Girls (like Girl Scouts, but through our church), gymnastics and baton. Needless to say we do quite a bit of running!!

This summer, Mali learned how to swim and also experienced camping for the first time as we packed up and went on our first family camping trip with some of our family. Mali and Joey thought the huge three-room tent was pretty neat! We plan to do a lot more camping next summer. We also met up with Tom's family in August for our second annual Wisconsin Dells get together. We enjoyed the water parks and Mali's favorite activity — go-karts!

The biggest change this year was a new school. After much prayer, we decided to move the kids to a wonderful Christian school. It's been so neat to see Mali's faith blossom through all that she learns and experiences. Though initially the change was challenging, just a short time, she became acclimated and is friends with all of the girls in her class. In fact, her second grade teacher (who is a wonderful Christian woman) says that Mali is the person that the girls turn to help mend problems that come up. They all look to her as the mediator! We're very proud to report that she earned eight A's and one B on her first report card. Considering that the academics are almost a year ahead of where she was last year, that's quite an accomplishment!

It is so wonderful to see her reading, writing in cursive, doing math, telling time, etc.! The only hurdle she has is that she is a perfectionist, which slows her down sometimes, but she's trying hard to overcome this!

This October was a highlight as my parents took all of us to Disney World. As you can see, we had a wonderful time. We spent a few days in the actual park. I think we saw almost all of the characters! Mali's favorite was Magic Kingdom – especially Winnie the Pooh – who (along with her other love – koala bears) has become near and dear to her. Needless to say, she was "Pooh" and "koalaed" out at Christmas!

We wrapped up the year at the kid's Christmas program where Mali was a baton-twirling angel. When Mali and Joey, with their classes, sang "Silent Night" in Spanish and then went on to sing so many wonderful songs about our Lord's birth, we knew we had made the right decision with the new school!

Tom continues to be busy with his business and men's Bible study group; I, still working, (hopefully not too much longer!) am involved with an infertility and adoption support group (co-leading for two full years).

I share our story a lot – it's such a blessing that our adoption experiences give hope to others.

We hope and pray, Lois, that you have a blessed 1999!

Love,

Tom and Karen

January 5, 2000

Dear Lois,

Happy New Millennium! We hope that this time of new beginnings finds you and your family well!

We are very grateful that '99 is over! It's been a very challenging year for us! Tom's business closed in October, so it's been an up and down year! The good part (actually the best part) is that we relied on our faith to get us through the challenges and He responded—we are very blessed that our family has grown in both faith and with each other!

Even though it sounds like the same broken record every year, it's been another year of unbelievable changes for Mali!! Where have nine years gone?

1999 started out with a huge gymnastics party at the YMCA with Mali and twelve of her friends! Yes, she is the social butterfly - her social calendar is far busier than ours!!

Second grade was a transition between public and now Christian school. Mali has to fight for her grades (she's very detailed and takes her time to do things), but as of first quarter in third grade – straight A's!!! Her best friends at school, Brooke and Mary, keep her smiling everyday!

When she's not in gymnastics, ballet or Sunday School, Mali is sure to be found at Pioneer Girls – our church's version of Girl Scouts. We had to choose between Brownies and Pioneers this year – Mom couldn't keep up with both!!

This summer I was able to spend a lot of vacation time home with the kids – I loved it! We went to Iowa for Tom's Dad's family reunion and had a lot of fun meeting all of the cousins' kids!

We got to do a lot of fishing this summer and Mali's other favorite sport – rollerblading!! She's quite the fancy roller-blader!

We took our first attempt at a slumber party in July – actually not we – I! Tom was gone that weekend (funny how that works!). She had a great time!

In August, we went to Door County with my folks for one long glorious week – we went to the beach, pool, whirlpool, ice cream parlor, etc. I think you get the picture!

Third grade was another transition! Mali begged for her second grade teacher again, but finally accepted her new teacher and I have a feeling, we'll report the scene again next year!

October was a great month. Some dear friends of ours from Minnesota (who now live in Atlanta) came for a visit. Mali and Megan have known each other since Mali was born and are longtime friends. They had a great weekend together – we're hoping to see them again soon.

Christmas was great – we did a lot of traveling and saw our families over the course of a week. Mali now knows the truth about Santa and took great pleasure in carrying on the tradition for Joey this year.

Mali is such a loving and compassionate big girl! She's almost four feet tall and weighs about 65 lbs. She's not a morning gal, but a night owl through and through! She's acquired an appetite this year and is starting to eat us out of house and home – such an unusual event for her!

She loves koala bears – we try to find unique koala gifts each year! On the 15th we (as a surprise) will be going to the zoo where she will be going in the koala area with the zookeeper and help to feed, weigh, and take care of a koala – we can't wait to see the look on her face!

On Friday (the 7th) she will be having six of her friends over for a slumber birthday party. She's very excited!

Well, it's been another incredible year! It seems that each year gets better and better! We pray that the Lord will bless you and your family this year and keep you in His loving care!

With love,

Tom and Karen

Our Chosen Children
(Written by Karen)

Through tears of sadness,
years with empty arms.
Hope and prayers without answers,
broken hearts wanting to be healed....

Then, as God always does, an unexpected answer.
A call - "Will you choose this baby for your own?"
We saw you born into the world, our perfect daughter.
We held you and held tight to our dreams and prayers finally answered.
God's answer - always perfect, never quite the way we thought.
Our circle of love continued to grow.

But God wasn't done with our family yet.
Another call – "Will you choose this baby for your own?"
We then saw you born into the world, our perfect son.
Into our hearts and into our lives forever.
God's answer - sweeter than we ever thought possible.
Our circle of love was now complete.

Our hearts, once heavy, are now filled with joy.
Hopelessness has been healed with faith.
What a plan God had for us!
To have chosen both of you to grow into our hearts and lives forever!

CHAPTER 6

A Daddy's Journey of Fatherhood (Tom)

It is my privilege to contribute to *Dear Lois*. Our adoption story has had great impact on everyone involved. The journey for me began long before our daughter, Amalie, and our son, Joseph, were lovingly placed in our arms when two selfless women, Lois and Ruth, chose us to parent our beautiful children.

I'm the eldest of four children; as a young boy, my family experienced the loss of two brothers from sudden infant death syndrome (SIDS). At an early age, I learned how precious life is and how devastating the loss of life is. In a sense the experience matured me early to understand that things don't always go as planned.

I was part of a very large extended family with many aunts and uncles as well as more than forty first cousins. Two of my father's siblings were adoptive parents. I remember being drawn to the fact that seven of my cousins were adopted; to me they were like any blood relative, and while growing up, I had a close connection with many of them.

I always imagined getting married and having a large family, probably six or more children. It was a natural aspiration due to my upbringing. What I learned later was that God had a different plan for my lovely bride, our family, and me.

I met Karen during my junior year in college. In a very short time, I knew she would one day be my wife, and we began discussing our plans to raise a large family. We married in 1986, purchased our first home in the Minneapolis area, and within a couple of years began trying to add to our family. After about a year, we realized something was wrong and sought medical advice. Upon receiving medical test results, we were informed that we both had infertility issues and that our dream of creating a biological child wasn't in the cards.

I'm a planner, and up to this point, everything in my life had gone according to plan. To learn I had been born with a defect that resulted in sterility was devastating to Karen and me. In this culture we are raised as men to be able to fix things when they break or go wrong. I felt completely helpless to fix this "problem." I also felt humiliated and punished by God for whatever sin I'd apparently committed and for which He hadn't forgiven me.

I remember meeting with a doctor who told me women will do anything to have a child and I had a serious problem on my hands. This comment only added to the stress we were under in dealing with an issue that was very personal and private. I felt the situation was so unfair, and I was filled with hopelessness and loneliness without a place to turn. I asked Karen whether she would eventually leave me because of my inability to father a biological child. She responded in love and told me she would stand by me as she had promised in our wedding vows.

Eventually, we came across an infertility support group, Resolve, we began attending. Although most of the couples were much older than us (we were in our mid-twenties), participating helped to normalize the situation for us as we were able to share the experience with others dealing with the same crisis. As we set our eyes on the future, we began discussing adoption and different forms of infertility treatment. The outcome was that we selected an anonymous donor for artificial insemination to achieve a pregnancy. While I couldn't provide the means of fathering a biological child, at least I could participate at doctors' appointments and assist in selecting the donor. Our solution to the problem wasn't necessarily normal, at least to me, but it was a way to "fix the problem" and achieve our goal of becoming parents, which we both greatly desired.

The infertility process was lengthy with many peaks and valleys emotionally and medically. It seemed that Karen and I were never on the same page at the same time. I'm sure our sheer stubbornness to achieve the common goal of a pregnancy was what kept us going at times. As time pressed on without achieving a pregnancy, we began to discuss adoption as an option. In the summer of 1990, we reached out to family, friends, and any medical staff or clergy members we could think of to share our desire to become parents. To our surprise, in early fall we were informed that Karen was pregnant, and we thought our problems were behind us. The pregnancy lasted for about two months, at which time the doctor told us it was no longer viable. We suffered yet another loss.

Reeling from the loss of our first child, we pressed on to pursue parenthood. As we needed to take time off from infertility treatments, we refocused our energies on pursuing adoption and let our contacts know what had happened. Unfortunately, as I found out in later years, I completely left my bride, Karen, behind as she continued to struggle with the loss of our pregnancy. My role was to "fix the problem," and mentally I pressed on without her.

In late December of 1990, we received a phone call from my cousin Pat, who had a friend, Lois, who was pregnant and due to deliver any day. She said Lois would like to meet us and was strongly considering us to be the parents of the child. We met Lois on December 29, 1990, in New Ulm, Minnesota, at Pat's home. I was filled with anxiousness, not knowing what to expect. Thankfully, Lois put us at ease and almost immediately asked us to be her child's parents; she invited us to be present in the delivery room. This offer caught us so off guard that we couldn't give her an answer. We spent hours with Pat, Lois, and her children, Bryan and

Jenaya. The experience was surreal, and when we left them later in the afternoon, we told Lois we would get back to her.

As we drove back to Minneapolis that day, Karen fell asleep during the ride. I remember being confused and silently reaching out to God for answers. I believe this was the first time I had ever listened for a response from Him in my life. When Karen awoke, I told her about my conversation with God and said that He had a plan for us. Lois needed a good family for the child, the child needed a family who would love him or her, and we desperately needed a child to love. There was no way to say no to this opportunity. God had laid this situation right in our laps! When we got home, we immediately called Lois and accepted her offer to allow us to adopt her child.

For two weeks we waited on pins and needles until we got the call from Lois on January 13, 1991, that she would be induced the next day and that our child would be born into this world. On January 14, we drove to New Ulm early in the morning to meet her at the hospital. It was an extremely cold Minnesota day, but that didn't matter to us. This day would change our lives forever!

When we got to the hospital, we were escorted to the maternity floor and suited up with hospital garb. We were made to feel comfortable and not just as bystanders. We spent the entire day with Lois as we waited for this child to come into the world. I felt so close to this woman, Lois. The bond was vast then and still is to this day. It developed so quickly because of her selfless act to choose life for this child in spite of circumstances for her that were incredibly difficult, I am sure. On top of that, she chose *us* to be the parents of this precious life she was bringing into the world. Karen teases me because I acted nervously, as any expectant father would, on delivery day. As Lois walked the halls on the maternity floor to pass the time and to allow the baby to drop to the birth canal, I anxiously followed behind her with a wheelchair, just in case!

At 1:17 p.m., Karen and I witnessed the birth of our beautiful little daughter, Amalie (Mali) Elizabeth Schlindwein. Her birth and the birth of our son are absolutely the most awesome experiences I've had, ones I will remember all my life. Upon her delivery, Mali was placed in her mother, Karen's, arms, and I was overjoyed to witness this moment. Lois smiled and said, "You are her parents!" This was a gift few people will ever experience, the selfless act of a loving birth mother handing a brand-new baby to adoptive parent forever. I guess I probably didn't realize it then, but God is good. We stayed in the hospital that day as long as we could and then traveled back to Minneapolis to purchase an outfit to bring our "Mali Dolly" home in the next day.

January 15th was at least as cold as Mali's birthday. We traveled back to New Ulm to pick up our daughter and say good-bye to Lois. Departing from her was bittersweet. I knew at that time that we would probably never see her again, and leaving her behind was difficult because of the close connection we had with her. On the other hand, I was struck with the awesome responsibilities of becoming a daddy. The bond with Mali was immediate, and Karen and I instantly fell in love with her.

Introducing Mali and Joey to our friends and family brought some of our proudest moments. Everyone embraced them immediately. These were exciting times—remodeling the nursery and learning how to feed, burp, change, and bathe infants. We were like any family with clothes to wash, bottles to sterilize, careers to juggle—and being parents. The best part of being Mali and Joey's dad was relearning what it was like to be a kid and witnessing all their firsts—relearning nursery rhymes and the lessons we all learned in kindergarten, such as "Wash your hands" and "Say 'please' and 'thank you'"; and watching them learn things for the first time. I have enjoyed *every* season of their lives, though admittedly some seasons more than others.

Fatherhood is unconditional; it is a gift God gives that cannot be undone. There is nothing my children can do to change that I'm their father and that I love them. My love for Mali and Joe is infinite, and I often wonder whether I would have been the same father if

Karen and I had been biological parents. We don't take anything for granted, and I might have done so in a different situation. We have been blessed by these two incredible gifts from God and from Lois and Ruth.

Being a dad has taught me a lot about my heavenly Father. He, too, is my adoptive Father. I am His chosen child, just as Mali and Joe are my chosen children. I once told them that I will always be their dad, and this is true. Nothing can change that—not even death or separation. After their adoptions were finalized, our status would never change. This is how it is with God. He has adopted us as sons and daughters into His family and has promised never to leave us or forsake us. He chooses us similarly to how Karen and I chose Mali and Joe. They didn't have a choice; they couldn't choose us because in their infant state, they didn't have the capacity to do so. This is how it is with God the Father. He chooses us because we don't have the capacity to choose Him; we would likely choose someone or something else. Thank You, God, for teaching me Your ways through being a father to my children. There's another great gift from Him.

Our adoption experience with Joe was very similar to Mali's. About a year after we brought Mali home, we contemplated how to grow our family. We quickly dismissed infertility treatment and all the associated stress; we again put the word out that the three of us were looking to grow our family. After one failed attempt with a birth mother, a pregnant birth mom named Ruth contacted us; she was due in several months to give birth to a child she felt unable to parent. As time pressed on, the three of us were excited to welcome yet another baby into our home.

On June 16, 1993, our bundle of joy arrived in Elgin, Illinois. Like our first delivery experience, we traveled to the hospital that morning and spent the day with Ruth as she prepared for delivery. Throughout the months of pregnancy and the hours in the delivery room, we developed a strong bond with another selfless, loving woman. That evening Karen and I witnessed the beauty of the birth of our son, Joseph Thomas Schlindwein, whom I named after a very close and deceased cousin. Joey was another gift from God, and our life would never be the same again. Now I was a daddy the second time to a bouncing baby boy. What joy we all had in our hearts to bring him home!

Looking back. I feel blessed to have had all these experiences in my life. While we struggled in the beginning, Karen and I are convinced that God worked out our adoption story for our good and His glory. We certainly didn't understand the path He took us down in the beginning, but we understand now what a blessing He has been in our lives and what a blessing Mali and Joe have been to us and countless others.

Praise be to God!

CHAPTER 7

I'm a Doggy, and I'm Special! (Karen)

Amalie and Joe have always known they were adopted; there wasn't a specific date or event when we told them about their adoptions. We began telling their stories to them before they could talk, read, or walk. Adoption has been a natural part of their lives for as long as they can remember. We tried to help them learn that adoption was as normal as breathing. We were well aware of the negative feelings some people had about adoption and wanted to be sure their story would be a strength they could embrace. We taught them that we had chosen them and that they were, therefore, our chosen children; they were never made to feel different, only loved. As Joe says,

> Since I was a baby, I was always taught that I was chosen by God to be with a family who cares about me and can support me. When I was little, I didn't really process what it meant to be adopted very much, so didn't really understand what adoption was to me until I grew up. Now that I'm an adult, I realize that adoption is more than being moved to a different family.

We had a few children's adoption books that became part of our normal bedtime stories, and we talked openly and freely about adoption from the moment they were both born. As we rocked them to sleep as infants, we told them about the special way they had been brought to us. We let them know about the special women who had made the choice for us to be a family. We taught them that adoption is special.

While we were looking to adopt our second child, a woman from our church wrote a series of articles for a local newspaper to share our networking adoption story. She interviewed all of us to help share our story and generate support for our mission. When she asked Mali what she thought of being adopted, her response (a rendition of it) was, "I'm a doggy, and I'm special!" At two years old, she hadn't yet mastered pronouncing the word *adoption*; "a doggy" seemed to explain exactly what she meant.

I recall a day at a new elementary school when, in second grade, Mali let her teacher know about her adoption. Mali was in a panic when I picked her up, as her teacher wasn't quite sure she was telling the truth. Both of our kids have such an uncanny resemblance to Tom and I that most people, had they not known, would never have guessed they were adopted.

A few years later I overheard a friend ask Mali who her "real" mom was. Mali understood at a very young age that she had a birth mother *and* a mother. She very calmly said, "My mom is my real mom." Mali understood that both of her mothers were real—one had nurtured her to bring her into this world, and one had nurtured her once she was in this world. She has always had a great respect for Lois and her decision for placing her with us.

When the kids were young, I cofacilitated the Hope Ministry (an infertility and adoption support group). During those years our lives were interwoven with adoptive families, many of who were going through or had completed the adoption process. There was even one close friend who is an adult adoptee. We had many events with our extended adoptive "family" and those going through infertility. Our kids interacted with each other often. There came a time when both Mali and Joe thought it was strange for someone *not* to be adopted!

Both of our kids had their own responses to adoption. Mali was so transparent that she would tell everyone who would listen to her story. At points in time, we reminded her that being an adopted child didn't define her but that she had been given a gift. Joe, on the other hand, rarely talked about his adoption, though he was very engaged with our adoptive friends. In the past couple of years, he has expressed a possible interest in finding his birth family; should he decide to follow through on that desire, we will happily assist him.

> Searching for my biological parents is a curiosity of mine and it comes and goes. I am not really sure that is something that I want to seek out as I am content with the family that I have. I was told my birth-story from my parents as I was growing up so I know what had happened through the process of my adoption. I feel as though I have enough information to process my story.   - Joe

When both Mali and Joe turned eighteen, we let them know that our agreement with their birth parents was for Mali and Joe to choose whether to pursue meeting them. Mali was so secure in who she was that she didn't have a missing identity as many adoptive children do. While we'd hoped she would perhaps make that choice someday, it was always up to her (and Joe), not to us.

CHAPTER 8

Reflections on Infertility and Adoption (Karen)

Just the word *infertility* transports me back to a very challenging time in life and in our marriage. *Yahoo Dictionary* defines *infertility* as "the persistent inability to conceive a child." The reality of the inability to conceive left me helpless and hopeless. Because of infertility, I was helpless to achieve a pregnancy women around me could, helpless to have control over my body and cause it to do something I'd dreamed of since I was young. Overcoming this struggle warranted medical tests, exams, treatment, and difficult, expensive choices that often resulted in the same disappointment month after month and put us further into financial debt. I had little hope that we would ever have a baby.

Infertility elicited advice from people who had little understanding of our circumstances. Had doctors told us that going on long vacations would cause a pregnancy, we would have sold everything and sojourned the world. Had medical support proved that getting rid of day-to-day stress would achieve our dreams, we would have gladly quit our jobs, sold everything, and lived a meager lifestyle. Had we had the finances to invest in every vitamin, supplement, and drug we were told would "work," we would have gone into further debt to try anything and everything possible.

All the newspaper articles, magazine stories, and books that were passed along to us had information that had led to someone getting pregnant and having a baby, but those stories weren't our story. In God's plans for building our family, we weren't that couple who'd achieved an easy pregnancy by following the "how to" suggestions.

For me infertility meant isolation. It was isolation from experiencing the joy friends had discovered in a pregnancy, isolation from having my own baby shower when I was attending one after another for those we knew. It was isolation from others who couldn't understand the pain I experienced that my body had failed me in being able to achieve a pregnancy. Our marriage also suffered its own isolation. We went through difficult treatments that for me were all consuming, with the highs of anticipation to the lows of disappointment. We were often on a different page during the journey; one of us would be ready to give up, while the other would plant his or her feet firmly and not move. It was necessary for me to talk about infertility— frequently. It was necessary for Tom to try to "fix it," and when he couldn't, he would try to push past it.

Because I had little faith during our journey, infertility was also isolation from God. I cried out to Him, begging Him to bring us a baby. Having a baby was my focus, fixation, and obsession. Years later I came to understand the magnitude of His love that had allowed me to experience all these feelings; it was only because of all these feelings that I could ever really understand the love He had for me and the love I could have for these miracles He'd put in our lives.

In 1992, I was the newsletter editor for *Resolve of the Twin Cities*. My daddy, Walter, agreed to write this article for one of the publications. While today dementia has taken much of his memory away, his words back then are what he would say today.

> This article is submitted as a tribute to our kids – daughter Karen and her husband, Tom. We have deeply admired their courage and resolve to overcome the emptiness of their earlier childless

marriage. Their determination to fill that void in their lives achieved a climax with the successful adoption of a beautiful daughter, Amalie.

Little Mali, now approaching two years old, has brought much joy to all of our lives, especially we, the grandparents, with our newly acclaimed titles of "Nana" and "Papa". It would seem, at this point, that this story should stop with a fairy tale ending, "they lived happily ever after." However, while we all share in the immediate happiness of the moment, theirs was not all without the traditional pain and suffering and the accompanying disappointment, frustration, and anxiety of not knowing when or what the ending might be. It is for these reasons that we prepared this contribution, relating our experiences that they would in some manner alleviate the concerns, fears and guilt that so many subject themselves to in their endeavor to become parents.

We were introduced to infertility problems early in our own marriage. Following the birth of Karen we, as many others, were unable to further expand our family. We, too, sought medical attention with the accompanying testing, counseling, and advice, all of which proved to be unsuccessful.

Subsequently, we redirected our efforts towards adoption, seeking information from numerous agencies. Following years of submitting applications, attending review meetings, and unanswered correspondences, we abandoned that unsuccessful effort.

Our void was, to an extent, fulfilled following our enrollment into a foster parenting program. Unfortunately, we gave up on that since we were unable to adjust to the separations each time a child was taken and placed (we had our first foster child for fourteen months). Little did we realize that the experiences we were exposed to would regenerate in our "golden years" as a resource for our kids, Tom and Karen.

During one of our trips to visit them they introduced us to their plight of childlessness, which we had suspected. Because of our closeness and family unity, they confided in us to learn from our experiences as they told us of their problem and their plans and objectives to fulfill their biological shortage. We were, at first, taken back by the introduction of new high tech terms, medical procedures, etc., which we were unfamiliar with. Tom and Karen were, however, quite sincere in wanting to know our feelings and attitudes about these "new" solutions to childlessness.

As we pondered and learned more about these solutions and formed our attitudes in relation to them, it became quite apparent that their emptiness was just as ours was; their search for a solution was just as ours was but their resolve and courage was far greater than ours. It then became our conclusions that we could, with some adjustment of our attitudes, provide a valuable service to them by giving them the support and cooperation so vital in their efforts to achieve their goal. We were now in a position of rekindling that all-important family support that we, too, had been recipients of.

We remember the great concern we had with infertility treatment that Karen underwent, realizing her discomfort, the extensive costs, and the unknown risks involved. We recall the joy of learning that this treatment culminated in a successful pregnancy only to have it end in disappointment with the tragedy of a miscarriage.

With that new emptiness and time running away and with "success becoming more elusive," they redirected their efforts towards adoption. Following numerous meetings with adoption agencies, they realized the odds of success there. Their next and final success was achieved through designated adoption. It was there with their tenacity and determination, using their creative prowess that moved them forward to the successful adopting of little Mali, our pride and joy. All of that success was generated in only a few short months.

Now as the months have rolled by, we have seen the love and excitement that has been brought into their lives, as well as ours, with their gift from God, who is truly theirs and ours to love and care for. Because of these experiences, we have all learned where there is hope, patience, faith, family support, and bonding, there is also the reward of success.

What I say next has surprised many people over the years. I honestly would go through every minute of pain, fear, and hurt all over again to have Mali and Joe. Infertility was the journey that shaped the person I am today. This was a time that tested our marriage; we experienced the "in sickness and in health" part of our vows early on and persevered. Infertility allowed me to better appreciate my children in a way I don't think I would have had we not gone through the battles we did to have them. Most importantly, infertility was the first time I paid attention to, and longed to hear from, God. It was the start to the most important journey of my life.

CHAPTER 9

Our Hope Is in the Name of the Lord (Karen)

Infertility allowed us very little control in our plight to have a family. Since by nature we are controlling individuals, it was a challenging journey for us. Tom is a reflective thinker; I'm a reactionary doer. A challenge like infertility for a young marriage could be a recipe for disaster. We were often not on the same page; Tom wanted to try to fix the problem, which he couldn't fix, and I wanted to talk about it all the time.

As there weren't too many life experiences for us to draw on to get through those days, I knew I needed some help. I turned to Resolve, a national infertility and support network. I immersed myself in support groups and meetings, and I eventually volunteered. As a volunteer, I found that helping others through their struggles helped to put my own into perspective. There were many stories far more challenging than our own. Helping others helped me to channel some of my energies toward doing something productive. Eventually, I became the newsletter editor for our local Resolve branch.

After Joe was born, my faith journey began, and our church connected me with Miriam, who quickly became a good friend. Like me, she and her husband had experienced infertility and then adoption, and she desired to help struggling couples go through the experience with support, encouragement, and hope. Through this connection, the Hope Ministry began. Our mission was to support, encourage, facilitate, and educate couples who were experiencing infertility and seeking resolution. For eight years we held monthly informational meetings, Bible studies, and different fellowship events. We saw dozens of babies and children arrive both biologically and through adoption. The stories were miraculous, the losses painful. As a group (our extended family), we walked through the difficult pain for some and the joyous family additions for others. We walked together, as God intended; God was indeed in the midst of that group.

I was blessed to have been in the midst of situations that stretched me, ones that drew on our own experiences; they allowed me to help others through their circumstances. God took one of the darkest parts of my life and used it for His glory. What an honor and blessing that ministry was to my family and me. As Mali and Joe were part of a network of so many adopted children, they truly grew up with a clear understanding of the process. They joined in welcoming child after child brought to us through adoption into our extended family.

> Being around other adopted kids, as I was growing up, was helpful because I could relate to them in a way that I couldn't with other people. My relationship with my sister has nothing to do with our being adopted; we are a brother and sister just like anyone else. And even though when I was growing up I was confused, at times, about adoption, I know that Mom and Dad are my "real" parents. I've never felt different because I'm adopted instead of biological. I look a lot like my Dad, so it's never been an issue for me. -Joe

Over the years, family, friends, and strangers have asked me for advice on different infertility and adoption issues. Friend-of-a-friend connections are made, and I continue to experience the joy of being able to listen, knowing that I have a great God who will guide me through the process of helping someone. Several years back, I had the great joy of connecting two families together to form an adoption plan (this little girl is so special to our family that she was the flower girl at Mali and Jason's wedding). I am amazed by how God has used me, and continues to do so, in this area of my life. For me serving has been a blessing and something I hope to continue doing for years to come. My faith grew abundantly from seeing God's handiwork, which is so evident, and from seeing so many living their faith through this journey.

As part of our ministry, we wrote materials for our Hope publication, which offered the hope found in the foundation of our faith; this excerpt shares the heart of what we taught and the message of hope God led us to provide.

> "But as for me, I will always have hope; I will praise you more and more." —Psalm 71:14 (NIV)

There are over one hundred sixty references of the word "hope" in the Bible. The first two references, found in the Old Testament, talk of seemingly "hopeless" situations. Naomi (Ruth 1:12 NIV) in addressing her daughter-in-law, Ruth, said, "Even if I thought there was still hope for me..." Ezra (1Chronicles 29:15b NIV) writes about David's prayer to the Lord, "Our days on earth are like a shadow, without hope."

Just as Ruth and David talked of hopeless situations in the Old Testament, many who journey through infertility feel that same hopeless feeling today. How hard it is for our limited human minds to understand why infertility has intervened in our lives. For many, infertility can be a hopeless journey; one where faith is overcome by grief and the overwhelming desire to have a child.

It was these overwhelming feelings of hopelessness, frustration, and faithlessness that plagued me during our infertility experience. I did not understand that God desired a personal relationship with me; that He desired for me to accept His perfect gift of grace. It was when I accepted that He was Lord and Savior of my life that I began to experience the hope that He desired for me, and a peace that I had not known before. It was at that point in my life, that I had a desire to help other couples going through the infertility journey to not experience the hopelessness that I did.

"We wait in hope for the Lord; He is our help and our shield." —Psalm 33:20 (NIV)

Holding
Onto God's
Promises
Expectantly

CHAPTER 10

Adopted or Biological: Does It Matter in Our Family? (Karen)

Prior to adopting Mali, I think I feared that I would have a hard time loving an adopted child as much as I would a biological one. I wondered what I would think if my child didn't look like me; I wondered whether I would always be filled with an ache to have a biological child. I had heard the difficult stories—families unable to bond with adoptive children … Nothing could have been further from what our experience was. In fact, I would say that I don't think I could have loved a biological child as much as I could have loved these two children.

I've come to understand that God wrote the story of my life long before I entered the picture. He had all my days outlined and planned. He knew which children were to be written into the story of our lives. I know these were the children God had chosen for our family—not only because of two loving women but also because of my loving heavenly Father.

The first time I saw the face of our daughter was the first time God's love became real to me. By the time our son was born, I found the capacity to love again with an open heart, in a way I couldn't describe. Both of these precious lives are a reflection of the love God had for us. That He would weave Lois and Ruth into our lives to make their choices for us to become parents and then bring these two miracles to us is still beyond my human comprehension. I know I would have no ability to be able to create a more beautiful story than what God did.

Since I grew up with family and friends who were or had adopted, adoption wasn't a new idea to me. It was an alternative way to bring children into a family. While Tom was leap years ahead of me in realizing we should consider adoption during our infertility journey, once I got there, there were no doubts that this was how we wanted to build our family. After our miscarriage, we continued both infertility treatments and the pursuit of adoption at the same time. I suppose that my hesitation not to give up on the infertility treatments was due to the lingering desire to become pregnant and give birth; when I finally let go of that, it was the death of a dream, and I grieved. What I eventually came to realize was that my bigger dream was to have a baby, and the biological likeness to him or her wasn't my focus. Once I came to that reality, the adoption process was something I embraced.

For me, choosing adoption to create our family meant that I could finally regain some control I'd lost during infertility. It meant that I could send out letters, talk with family and friends, network, and "promote" ourselves to others to help us find an adoptive situation. I was able to control the degree of outreach we were able to do. For the first time in a long while, I had some say in the process, and I felt rejuvenated.

At the time, the process of designated adoption (a birth mother designating an adoptive couple) wasn't new, but the process of networking to be matched to a birth mother rather than waiting on a traditional adoption list for a few years was somewhat new. We were pioneers on a new journey and bound and determined that we weren't going to wait for years without our baby. Our letters "let in" our closest family and friends to the emotional journey we had gone through. We were finally willing to allow transparency into our relationships to help explain our deep desire for a baby.

Our plea resulted in receiving our daughter, Amalie, four months earlier than our biological baby would have been born. Sometime after her birth, we returned to our specialist to consider infertility treatment once more; instead, we chose adoption to complete our family. The turmoil of infertility was our past; adoption was our present and future. Following the birth of our son, Joe, we both felt peace to know that our family was complete.

Once we chose Amalie and later Joseph, we never turned back. That they wouldn't be from our bloodline never overshadowed the excitement of becoming parents; I don't think either of us ever considered that. The fact that our kids both resemble us probably did make that part easier for us, but we never looked at them as being different from biological children.

I remember that my dad was hesitant during their first trip to meet Mali; he wondered how he would love this new baby. Any of his doubts were put to rest the moment he saw her. I'll never forget the first time he held her and soaked up the moment of realization that he loved this little one more than he thought possible. Tom's mom, Midge, shared special memories of becoming "Grandma" for the first time.

> When Amalie was born, "Grandma" was my new name and I was so proud to have that title! The day she was born I let everybody around me know that my first grandchild was here. Mali is my granddaughter and family and I love her!

Kim, a close friend, recalls the time when our daughters met for the first time; it was the start of a lifelong friendship.

> Our daughter Megan, from the day she was first introduced to Amalie, was so fascinated and excited

to now have someone to play with. As the days and months progressed Megan could not pronounce the name "Amalie" so she began calling her "Baby Mali." The chemistry was instant and they bonded like glue. Mali looked up to Megan as a big sister and Megan loved the role of being a big sister. It was an awesome friendship.

When I stop to think how very differently my family's life would have been if "Baby Mali" and Joe would never have been adopted and never been able to be a part of our lives for these past twenty-three years, I see how many blessings adoption can bring families.

Karen's mom, Lillian, was overcome with emotions during the car ride to see their little Mali for the first time.

I was excited and couldn't wait to meet our little granddaughter. There were many tears of happiness during that long car ride; we were anxious to get there; there was so much joy and excitement that this little girl came into our lives!

Adoption over the years was both a great blessing and a challenge. Just as we went through a variety of emotions, so did Lois's family. Jenaya explains,

Over the years, I remember people asking how many brothers and sisters I had. I would always tell them that I had five brothers and three sisters; if more was asked I would explain that some were half, some were step, and some were blood. I always included Amalie in that list. She is my sister and will always be and I was never shy about telling people about her. Most people assumed she was older than me, but I would kindly explain that she was actually younger than me by seven years.

It was always a shock and most people would express disbelief that Mom could have made that choice (adoption). I don't think they viewed placing a child for adoption as a horrible thing, but at times I knew I took it that way. I think most knew that my mom was such a caring person and would do anything for anybody; they were shocked that she could put her own child up for adoption after already having two children. In response, I would explain that my mom wasn't in the best situation to raise another child. She did what she knew would be best for the baby.

If my mom hadn't placed her for adoption, Amalie would have never had the experiences she did in life. She would never have played the piano or gone to Mexico to help build homes for people in need. She wouldn't be who she is today, if it wasn't for the placement with her parents, Tom and Karen.

I'd be lying if I said I never had negative feelings about the adoption. There were times I would cry while holding her pictures and wishing that I could have grown up with her. There were times I didn't understand how my mom could have placed her for adoption. She was my sister and I didn't know if I would ever meet her. It got to me at times, but then I'd reflect back to all she accomplished and achieved and it would help with my negative feelings.

In the end, the outcome has been one that I could have never imagined. With the loss of my best friend (my mom, Lois), to gaining an entire family

who has been there for us with open arms with what
I hope is a lasting relationship.

"Faith makes things possible, not easy" (Author
unknown). I truly believe this!

I firmly believe that because of what we experienced to get
Amalie and Joe, I'm a better parent. Tom and I have often said that
without the pain we endured, we don't know whether we would
have appreciated our children nearly as much as we do. We have
always greatly understood the sacrifice that was made for us to have
both of them, and the women who helped us build our family have
humbled us.

I wouldn't be truthful if I didn't say there were times over the
years when I feared my kids could be taken away from me. When
they were young, there were many adoptions in the news that
hadn't been finalized properly, and children were released back to
birth family members. As the years went on, I saw TV shows that
portrayed an "adoption reunion" of the adoptive child and the birth
family but not typically the adoptive families. I used to wonder
whether my kids would ever choose another family over ours.

There were times, while I was growing up, when
I would have an argument with my parents and
thought that finding my biological family would
cure the problem. I didn't go through with it as I
thought of the potential outcome of what that could
do to our family.   -Joe

There was no foundation for those fears, but they were on my
mind at points in time. Interestingly, Lois went through a similar
experience, as Jenaya remembers:

Actually there was a reality show that was on a
couple of years ago where adoptive families were

meeting birth families...and people always talked about forgiving the birth parent, etc. I think that Mom was thinking the same. I was kind of nervous when it came out because I KNEW my mom would watch it and I didn't want it to get her mind going, but, of course, she watched it and it did get her mind going a hundred different ways.

We were two mothers; we both loved our child, and both of us feared rejection. Recently, I shared with Jenaya that neither Mali nor we had any ill feeling about Lois and her decision. There was no forgiveness to be extended because she hadn't done anything to warrant it. *She* had done the gift giving; all of us knew that and admired her for her decision.

I often heard that birth mothers "gave up" or "gave away" their babies. Birth mothers don't give up or give away these precious lives. Rather, they entrust and place the lives of their babies with adoptive families. They put their needs aside for what they feel is best for that child.

We frequently heard the question "Who are their *real* parents?" as if we weren't living and breathing. Birth parents and adoptive parents are both very real. Birth mothers carry and nurture a baby until birth, and at some point in time, they decide to place their child with an adoptive family. The adoptive family raises and nurtures that child for the rest of their lives. Both families can love, and both have dreams for the child. I'm blessed to have two children who have been surrounded by adoption and understand that they aren't different but chosen. Both have expressed a possible desire to adopt in the future.

I would consider adopting a child someday because I've experienced good things with adoption and I could relate to a child's adoption experience.   -Joe

Infertility was the valley in our marriage that caused both of us to hear God's voice for the first time. Adoption became the mountaintop experience God allowed us to journey to find the children He had chosen for us. We have been blessed because of the love of two women who chose life for them. Adoption became my passion, and I thank God for both infertility and adoption, which have shaped my heart and molded me into the person I am today.

January 1, 2001

Dear Lois,

We hope this letter finds you healthy and happy at the start of 2001!

2000 started out by Mali and Joey joining in on the new millennium celebration until after the stroke of midnight – they were very excited!

On her ninth birthday, we traveled to the zoo as a surprise for Mali. We met the koala (her favorite animal) zookeeper behind the scenes and Mali got to help take care of, feed and touch RT, the koala. She was a very happy nine year-old! The celebration continued with a slumber party with a few of her closest friends.

The last celebration was a treat from her Nana when we took a lunch trip to the American Girl Doll Factory in Chicago. I've never seen her eyes so wide as they were as we walked through the doll shops!

We celebrated Mali's Grandpa's sixtieth birthday this spring with a family get together in Iowa and, later in June, her other Grandpa (Papa) celebrated seventy years of age with a surprise family party at our house.

Gymnastics lessons start again in a few weeks and Mali is anxious to begin. In our spare time (as you can tell, there's not much of that!) we also enjoy scrapbooking together.

Mali's fourth grade class has around twenty-five kids and the same teacher as last year. Though we've discovered that Mali has ADD (attention deficit disorder), she gets all A's and B's and fights hard to do well. The most significant thing that we have seen is how strong Mali's faith has become. She loves telling people about Jesus!

Choir and Pioneer girls at church fill up our other spare time. We are very involved with our church and Mali's faith has grown due, in part, to all of these experiences.

We continue to thank you for this precious gift. Mali and Joey are our chosen children and we thank you and our heavenly Father for the privilege of being their parents.

God bless you, Lois!

Love,

Tom and Karen

January 4, 2002

Dear Lois,

We hope this finds you and your family in good health. We hope you had a very blessed celebration of our Lord's birth.

This year (well, 2001…) started out with a ten year old birthday celebration. You counted it right – thirteen girls in all for a slumber party! As you can see, they had a lot of fun – sleep was not plentiful!!

In February, Mali had her first communion. There was a beautiful ceremony in our chapel – about one hundred fourth and fifth graders (whose parents felt were ready) communed with their kids in a very beautiful service.

Both last spring and starting again this fall, Mali is still involved with Pioneer Girls at church. They had a lot of activities that kept them busy and, most importantly, strengthened their faith. She will be taking babysitting training next month at church; she can't wait!

She has also started her third year of piano lessons. She had her second recital (having won an award for the second year in a row) this spring. She's done a great job with her practicing, though she doesn't think that she plays as well as she does.

Gymnastics is continuing. Vaulting is Mali's strength. She is in a pre-team class at the YMCA and will, if she wants to, probably have an opportunity to try out for their team in the next year or so.

This summer we took a trip to northern Wisconsin in a resort area we love to go to. We spent the week mini golfing, fishing, swimming, skipping rocks, building sand castles, go-karting and eating! We went with Karen's *folks and had a wonderful time! We all got new bikes in 2001 and had a chance to take a long bike hike through a beautiful state park!*

August was a busy month. Mali went back to Christian camp for a week (she did lots of crafts, swimming, rock wall climbing, etc.) during the hottest week of the year. We went up north again with friends for a long weekend.

The most special August event was the last week of the month when Mali and I reaffirmed our baptisms. Our church has a large outdoor pond and forty of us were baptized. Mali has a faith in the Lord that is so strong and so beautiful to see in a child.

In September, we took our annual Iowa trip to see Grandpa and came home with a new arrival – Zeke (Zacchaeus), our new puppy. He joins fourteen year-old Einstein. It's been great to see the kids with a puppy. Einstein was our baby before Mali and Joe.

This fall was on to fifth grade. The kids continue in the Christian school. What a blessing! She was on the volleyball team for the first few months and enjoyed that. She is getting all A's and B's – school seems to be getting easier this year (though harder for us!).

For Halloween, at Mali's request, she dressed as an angel and Joe as Moses. They went to only a few houses for candy; before they left (again, at Mali's doing) she told every neighbor that Jesus loved them! I cried when she told me – how beautiful she is – outside and in!

In November, our best friends from Atlanta visited and Mali got to spend time with her best friend.

Christmas is gone for another year, but the joy will not leave us. We feel so lucky that she still holds hands with us and hugs us – I savor every moment. She is really growing up – no longer a little girl and very anxious to be big!

Bless you, Lois, for the privilege of this beautiful girl.
We pray that the Lord will keep you healthy and happy
in 2002.

Love,

Tom and Karen

January 5, 2003

Happy New Year, Lois!

We hope that the start of 2003 finds all of you healthy and happy!

I suppose there never has been a year where such noticeable changes happened with Mali. This certainly has been an action packed one for her. The thought of a teenager in the house next year is a big enough change that we're preparing as best as we can!!

We started 2002 with glasses, added braces this summer, and concluded the year with contacts (so she can see more while in gymnastics!)! She'll have her braces for another two years and ultimately will need a bridge as she doesn't have the normal permanent teeth that are next to her front teeth.

Piano lessons and recitals have continued – motivation to practice has been a challenge, but she plays very well when she puts her mind to it! She has also started to show more interest in vocals, having had her first solo (brief, but a solo) line in the spring musical. She says that the guitar is her next instrument, which we gave our blessing to so long as she sticks with piano for the rest of this year!

Gymnastics has been a large part of her life this year. She made the team at the YMCA, having had her first meet yesterday! Vaulting is her specialty – I take a deep breath and pray when I see her flip in the air! She practices twice a week for 2- ½ hours, so it's quite a commitment!

At school, she is now considered to be in the Junior High (sixth-eighth grade) and is doing well. She is very self-motivated this year and takes responsibility for her studies. She's maintained about a "B" average. She is the peacekeeper and prayer warrior for her classmates.

At church, she is involved weekly in Godsquad, which is a Junior High program. She is a teen helper in one of our three-four year old programs and loves working with kids. Her faith in Jesus is rock solid and she is not afraid to share her faith. I truly believe that she will do some kind of missionary work someday. We'll have to see where the Lord leads her! In August, she attended her last year at church Kid's Camp and had a ball. Next year she'll have another opportunity to go with the junior high kids.

Mali got her Red Cross certification for babysitting and has been regularly sitting for her brother. She loves earning the money and we enjoy some time together!

This summer we enjoyed a trip to Atlanta, Chattanooga, and the Smokey Mountains to sight see and visit friends. The mountains were beautiful and we got to enjoy walking over rapids and streams to get to the waterfall in the pictures.

Until next year...

Thank you for the joy of our daughter. To look into her eyes is to see a reflection of God's love.

Love,

Tom and Karen

"Be exalted, O God, above the heavens, and let your Glory be over all the earth." —Psalms 108:5 (NIV)

December 31, 2003

Dear Lois:

Happy New Year! We hope and pray that this finds you well!

Can you believe it – an almost teenager! We're both learning its good points and its challenges! The physical changes (and emotional) were the most drastic this year!

Gymnastics was the first part of the year. With five hours of practice each week and a Saturday meeting (usually a few hours from home) almost every Saturday for a few months, things got a bit hectic. Eventually Mali decided that the team was too competitive and she opted to retire in summertime. She was an awesome vaulter this season and placed with several medals in competition.

Onward and upward with volleyball at school. There was a short two month season, but it was fun and she was with her school friends, so was very happy! The team did extremely well, having won first place in their division finals. She still goes to her junior high ministry nights every week at church for Bible study and hanging out with friends.

Mali spends a lot of time with little kids. Whether at Sunday School teaching three-year olds, or babysitting, she loves being around little children. Her goal for the next year-and-a-half, is to earn $600 so that she can pay for half of her first mission's trip to Guatemala during her Spring Break in eighth grade. The school decided it was a good way to send off the eighth grade class and allow them to see another part of the world and, at the same time, bring Guatemalan children the gospel message. She is very much looking forward to that; we are too, though travel is always a concern, so likely one of us will go with as a chaperone.

Braces are still on, but should be coming off in a few months – she is very excited to be rid of them! She has started the teenage acne phase and we are seeing a dermatologist, but she is taking it in stride and doesn't let that get her down. Motivation is hard to come by these days... instant messaging on the computer seems to far surpass her desire to want to study. Though challenged with motivation, she is able to maintain A's and B's. She is such a bright young lady and just needs a little jump-start now and then...

We were fortunate to have gone to Florida for vacation this year, to visit Nana and Papa and were able to go to Busch Gardens for a day trip. We had a few other weekends away with family, but mostly stayed home to do some home decorating.

Piano lessons are still going, but desire is starting to fizzle. She would love to take up the guitar, but we are trying to encourage her to stay with the piano (actually to commit to it first), before she takes her hand at another instrument. She does a really great job (when she wants to!!) and has come so far!

Mali has so many friends (although Joey is more of an annoyance now than her buddy!) and would love nothing more than to talk with them on the phone and on-line all day every day! She is such a good-hearted person and is always concerned about fixing problems between feuding friends. Her friends look up to her for advice; she is a very compassionate and caring friend!

God bless you during 2004 and always. Thank you again for the privilege and blessing of being Mali's family.

In Christ,

Tom and Karen

January 3, 2005

Dear Lois,

Happy New Year! We pray that you had a blessed Christmas season!

Year fourteen! Incredible! This year Mali has transformed from a girl to a young woman. We treasure those times when she sits down and talks with us and spends time with us, because we know they will become fewer and far between. My most treasured times are on Saturday mornings when she and I go to our favorite coffee spots for a latte! It's just the two of us spending one on one time and is so very special.

We spent Spring Break '04 in Florida with my folks again. We spent a couple of days at Sea World and had a lot of fun watching the dolphin shows, feeding the fish and just having a lot of fun. The beach time was equally nice! Just eight days of relaxation and family time!

Over the summer Mali and I went to visit friends in Atlanta. Our daughters grew up together in Minnesota and are a couple of years apart. We had fun spending time together and doing fun mother/daughter activities!

We spent several days in northern Minnesota where Tom's sister and family have a cabin. The weather, unfortunately, was very cold, but we had fun anyway. During the one-day of warm weather, we had fun tubing, boating and other fun "cabin" stuff! Despite the fifty to sixty-degree weather after that, the kids insisted on braving the cold weather in the tubes; go figure!

Volleyball was the focal point of the beginning part of eighth grade this year. Mali's team had a two-month season where they finished first place in their conference, though they didn't fare so well in the conference

94

tournament. Mali had a lot of fun and developed a very strong serve by the end of the season. We're not sure if she will continue on in high school.

What she has continued on with (very begrudgingly!) is piano. Tom keeps reminding her that she will regret it if she doesn't keep on; they made a deal earlier last year that if she kept up the piano that she could start another instrument that she really wants — drums! I reminded Tom yesterday that his "deal" with her expires next week. I'm not sure how we're all going to acclimate to this new instrument; I'm only sure that a lot of patience and aspirin will need to be available! We are also trying to find an art studio where Mali can start private drawing lessons as she has a passion for sketching, drawing and painting.

Babysitting has been a good activity in the past year. You'll see Mali holding two small children in the group shot of children. The children are from our infertility and adoption support group. Many of them are adopted. The two that she is holding are ones that she baby-sits; they are six months apart (one adopted from Guatemala and the other a biological child). She has her hands full. You'll also see a close up of her and a little blonde haired boy. This is one of two in another family that she regularly sits for. Mali also continues to teach Sunday School to the preschool kids on Sundays.

School has been going well. We opened a new junior high building this year, so the kids have been in a brand new environment, which has been great. Mali says she is going to miss it next year! She is nervous about high school as most of her friends will not be going to the public high school that she is slotted to attend. We are encouraging her to get more involved with her church junior high group, where many of those kids go to her school. Orientation is coming up in a few weeks; we can't believe it! She will graduate from eighth grade in May.

The exciting upcoming event this year will be at the end of March/start of April. The eighth grade class will be taking a mission trip to Mexico. They will be making homes for some of the poor village families who live in shacks. She is extremely excited to be going and has already raised most of the $1,000 fee through her babysitting and saving. Tom will be going with the group as a chaperone.

Have a safe and prosperous New Year. May the Lord bless you and your family! Thank you for the treasure you have placed in our lives.

Love,

Tom and Karen

WHERE JOURNEYS LEAD
(Written by Karen)

Your journey led you to nurture a baby inside your womb.

Your love led you to choose another family to provide for its needs and be able to help your dreams for this baby to come true.

Our journey led us to empty arms.

We hoped for the day we would have children to love, to provide for their needs, to be able to dream for them and love them throughout their lives.

It was nothing short of a miracle that caused our journeys to meet.

God wove our lives together so that we could accept the gifts that you gave to us and live out our dreams.

We will be forever grateful for the blessings that your love allowed us.

We will never forget the decision that was made that allowed our dreams to come true.

CHAPTER 11

Growing Up with Foster Children (Karen)

I'm one of the blessed. Though I came from a very small family, it was the fiber and foundation I drew from when we had our children. But my experience of growing up in a very small family was vastly different from what many people may have experienced. As an only child, I had a good relationship with my parents, my grandmothers (both of my grandfathers died before I was born), and my small extended family. Family get-togethers were frequent celebrations of birthdays and holidays. I can't imagine going through life without a tight-knit family.

When I was a young child, an older couple at our church was well known to the congregation because of the many foster children they toted with them each week. Sometimes they had several children at once; sometimes they had only the one boy, who lived with them for several years. Some of their kids came from situations involving drugs and abuse, and there were so many stories. When my parents took the leap of faith and decided to become foster parents, I was very happy to have little babies in our home. I didn't realize at the time that those babies were also helping to fill a void in my parents' lives after they were unable to conceive a second child. I was eleven years old when our first foster child, Tim, came to stay with us as a six-week-old infant.

> We went into fostering as we felt there was a missing link in our family. We found that there was a bond to these babies and that Karen loved having the babies around, so it was an experience that made us a stronger family.   –Nana Lillian

Little did we know that our first experience as a foster family would be the longest we had during the three years when we cared for these babies. Tim became the closest person I had to a brother as I was growing up. Legal issues caused a lengthy delay in his adoption process, but my parents made an intentional decision to keep him with our family until these challenges were resolved, as they wanted to provide him with stability rather than move him to another interim foster home.

By the time Tim left, fourteen months after we took him in, we were beyond attached to him, and his loss was as if someone in our family had died. A very loving family adopted him, and we were blessed to be able to see him over the next few years. In fact, I still have the blessing of keeping in touch with him via Facebook, and I recently talked with him. What a privilege God has given our family to be able to know how Tim is doing in his life.

After Tim, we took in seven more babies (Jamie, Johnny, Charlie, Kevin, JJ, Buddy, and Jason). Most of them were with us for short periods, from a couple of days to a couple of months. I greatly admire my mom, who adapted to each new baby, waking up during the night for most of the time they were with us. She did this eight times in a three-year period. There was a lot of love we shared with those babies, and it is clear to me now that God was very much preparing me for our future adoptions.

Fostering opened my heart to a new understanding of family. The attachment we developed to these babies in such a short time caused me to realize that biology wasn't necessary to form a bond of love. Fostering prepared both me and my parents to be able to readily love our kids, whether they were biological or adopted.

December 30, 2005

Dear Lois,

Happy New Year! We trust that you had a blessed Christmas this year! Well, though we sound like broken recordings every year, this is the year of the most change in Mali's life. This is by far the year that took Mali from child to young woman!

Following her Fourteenth Birthday Bash (everyone from her eighth grade class was invited – electric guitars, drums – which she started herself in January - and all!) Mali set her eyes towards the mission trip that she and Tom took in April to Reynosa, Mexico, for her eighth grade class trip. There they spent 7 days in a Texas Christian camp and were transported daily to a poor village in Reynosa. The team of 35 built three houses and held a daily Vacation Bible School. Mali loved being able to be with the children, as you can see, and using her Spanish skills. This trip impacted her life in a significant way. So much, in fact, that we have decided to repeat this trip with the school in 2006 as a family. This time we will be building more homes and have a team of fifty-two returning to a village in Reynosa. We are very excited and know that this will be an event that will have a lasting impact on our family and each of us individually for the rest of our lives! God is good!

In May, Mali graduated in a beautiful ceremony at our church. She surprised us a few weeks before by telling us that she and her friend wanted to sing a duet at the ceremony. They selected a song, "Together", that I had accompanied my eighth grade choir in my graduation ceremony. Because the words were not meaningful for a Christian graduation, she and I reworded the song. They sang it beautifully – it was the start of her realization that she likes to sing.

This summer gave us the opportunity of having a boat for the first time, so we spent a lot of family weekends on lakes and on the Mississippi boating, skiing, tubing, and camping. We had a lot of fun! We took the boat to Northern Wisconsin at a resort for a week with Grandma and had a great time of relaxation! Mali took her first solo flight to Georgia to visit one of her best friends whom she grew up with in Minnesota. They had a great time as her friend just got her license (ouch – that's coming soon for Mali as she'll start Driver's Ed this summer!)!

Mali's braces came off just in time for school and in the following weeks, bridges were added. She has a spectacular smile and, as you can see, is quite beautiful and quite grown up!

Mali joined the volleyball team prior to school starting, so had some friends on the team before her first day. Though she had a lot of difficulty accepting rude behavior from a few of her teammates, she stuck it out and grew quite a bit this year. We're not sure if she will join again, but we know she gained a lot from the experience.

Adapting to public high school wasn't as traumatic as we had thought. Mali connected up with a friend from third grade whom she hadn't seen for five years and has been connected to the hip ever since! She is a great Christian girl and they have both joined Fellowship of Christian Athletes, will be doing a dance class together, and have been talking about Mali joining their Christian band (Mali on drums!).

As a new public school student, one of the first benefits, outside of football and basketball games, was being able to go to a dance – finally, as Mali says! She was beautiful – she went with a group of friends – out to eat and then the dance. They had a great time!

Choir at school is one of the highlights; they just got done with their second concert prior to Christmas. They have recently sent home information about an upcoming trip in April, 2007 – China! The choirs, bands and orchestra will be taking a ten-day tour to several locations in China and performing along the way. She was very hesitant to go at first, but is now excited.

Babysitting and teaching Sunday School continue to fill her time. She constantly reminds us that she can get her temporary license this coming summer – we're in denial! She has uncovered a talent of writing poetry and has been asked by her English teacher to join the yearbook staff.

She has a 3.5 GPA and is doing well. She has her eyes set on a couple of small Christian colleges so we will be taking her to visit campuses this spring as she has asked to see them and we decided that it would be good incentive to keep her grades and goals in focus!

We hope all is well with you and your family. We pray that our Lord would watch over you and bless you in 2006! Thank you for the treasure we have in Mali.

God's blessings and love,

Tom and Karen

January 7, 2007

Dear Lois,

Sixteen? We cannot believe that Mali will actually be sixteen. Where does time go? We hope this is finding you well! We have had an incredible year!

Mali and I got to spend some time down in Florida in February with my folks. We had a great time relaxing, being warm, and spending quality time together. April was another great month. We, as a family this year, went to Reynosa, Mexico where we repeated the trip that Tom and Mali had taken in '05; this time all of us got to go. It was an incredible experience and we saw Mali growing up before our eyes. She related so well with the Mexican children as Vacation Bible School was led and as we built houses for four families. Her Spanish skills were used and stretched and she was amazing! It was such a great family experience that we have decided to go once more in April this year. Mali will be one of two alumni from the junior high school attending. She is a great mentor for the eighth graders!

Mali learned how to water-ski this summer after spending a great deal of time on our boat along the Mississippi and around many lakes. She especially likes the times that she could bring a friend with on the boat. In August we spent a week on the Mississippi with family and friends and on the boat (of course!). And in August we began an early college search. Mali has had her heart set on a Christian college for years; her dream is to be a teacher and journalist. We went to her first campus tour and she was ready to go!! We're not quite so sure how ready we are for her to go!! She's growing up way too fast.

Speaking of growing up — you guessed it. She got her driver's permit this summer and has been driving since. She'll actually get her license in March and has a car (Tom's car now) that she will get with the understanding that she is responsible for gas and insurance. Since she has great grades (3.8 GPA), she should be able to keep those expenses down! She is anxious to start looking for a job this summer.

Mali chose to not return to the volleyball team this year. There were many coaching challenges and team issues that she didn't want to be a part of. But God had a different plan for her. Rather than playing on a team, her junior high volleyball coach asked her and two of her friends, all alumni, to co-coach one of the junior high girls' teams. She was thrilled and had much fun leading this great group of girls.

This will be Mali's last year, we think, as a Sunday School teaching aide as she wants to be a full-blown teacher next year. She loves working with the small children and wants to be more challenged with them.

At school, she is in leadership with the Fellowship of Christian Athletes, attends a prayer meeting weekly with her FCA team, is on the yearbook staff (with hopes to become a Senior editor in a couple of years), is still in choir and is taking both drum and voice lessons. No wonder we're in the car all the time!! She still continues to go to youth group every week and babysits a lot! I wonder how much more she can squeeze in!!!

We pray that 2007 will be a blessed one for you and your family. Thank you for the joy that you have given us in Mali; she always has been and continues to be our miracle from you and from the Lord. May God richly keep watch over you!

Love,

Tom and Karen

December 30, 2007

Dear Lois,

Happy New Year! We hope that your Christmas season was filled with much happiness and joy!

2007 was by far the most change in Mali's life (and ours) that we have had yet; it seems hard to believe that in one more year she will be an adult, although she is so mature now that we have to be reminded that she isn't quite there yet.

January brought her (dreaded!) driver's license and car all in one month. She has been very responsible (although she did have her first small accident this summer – with no injuries) and we trust her as she has earned it with us! Around the same time, her first serious boyfriend entered the picture (this ended a couple of months ago but not until after the homecoming dance)... and this summer was her first job, working at a pizza party restaurant where she works as a children's party hostess... Wow!

We were able to do much traveling this year. We returned to Mexico for our third mission trip (we'll go once more this March) as it was Joey's eighth grade graduation trip... we were blessed with so many new friends and got reacquainted with some of the special ones from years past. As you can see, Mali is the center of the kids, where her heart is!

In May, Mali and Karen traveled to Georgia for the high school graduation of a family friend; we had a great time. In August, we traveled to Colorado where we got to see Pike's Peak, the Royal Gorge and Estes Park as well as horseback riding and white water rafting! It was a great trip.

Mali was inducted in the National Honor Society this fall; she continues to be in choir, is the junior yearbook editor, Sunday School teacher, praise and worship leader at her youth group (she is still taking voice lessons, though drums are no longer!), etc. She has narrowed her college search, thus far, down to two Christian Colleges. She plans to major in Christian Elementary Education and possibly minor in journalism. We are so blessed at the young woman she has turned out to be. She has a faith in Christ that is undeniable and wears a purity ring everyday as a commitment to wait for her future husband. She boldly stands up for truth and God at all times... She is amazing! It is going to be an adjustment to not having her around when she goes to college, but we know that she is ready for the challenge.

This past fall, Tom was diagnosed with prostate cancer, which was surgically removed along with all the cancer. We rejoiced and Mali absolutely grew in her faith from that experience. Karen had shoulder surgery in November, and continues to heal. Mali has been a tremendous help to both of us during our recoveries and we are very grateful (go figure!) that she has the ability to drive!

We will look forward to reporting about Mali once more next year when she embarks into adulthood. It seems like just yesterday when we were so blessed to have seen her enter the world and into our hearts... know how much each day with her has been an indescribable blessing to us...

With much love,

Tom and Karen

CHAPTER 12

The Last Letters

The last letters written to Lois and Ruth when our kids turned eighteen were the most difficult to write. How, in only a few pages, could we thank someone for a gift that is beyond anything else we had been given? How could we share the faith that has sustained us without knowing whether we would have an opportunity to share it again? How do we express our love and gratitude when our hearts are overflowing? I imagined how they would read those last letters. I wept. I cried out of gratitude because we had our family; I cried for them because they weren't able to see close-up the great people the children had become. I cried because I knew no more letters would be sent; therefore, I knew they would receive no more letters—at least not for now.

> I recall getting the "last letter", which was a very emotional time for our family. We knew that once Amalie turned eighteen we would no longer receive letters. I can honestly say I didn't want to open that envelope. I didn't want the letters to stop. I looked forward to them. I looked forward to seeing the entire family grow.

I remember the call from Mom saying the letter arrived. She was vague but I could tell she had been crying. She told me the next time I went to her house I could read it. I recall it asking her not to reach out to Amalie. She didn't understand why, but I did. I understood that it was Amalie's choice to reach out to her as it was Mom's choice to place her for adoption.

She tried to understand but still struggled with the "unknown". She would ask me if I thought she would want to meet her. I honestly didn't know. I didn't know if she ever would.

I hoped that because she was spiritual that she would have forgiven my mom and that she would have come to meet her. But it was wrong to assume that because she is spiritual and believed in God that she would reach out to her birth family. It was the only thing I could come up with to be hopeful that one day I may get the opportunity to meet her. As years went by, I started to think that opportunity was not going to happen. I had accepted it but my mom struggled with it. I truly believe that my mom was able to live with her choice because she was watching her grow up (through the letters) and once that stopped a piece of her just didn't want to accept it. She always said that if they had (Tom and Karen) not agreed to an "open" adoption, then she would not have done it. She needed to know what was going on in Mali's life to make peace with her decision.   — Jenaya

My mother took the eighteenth letter pretty hard and she was down and out for a while. I think she believed that she would always get letters and that maybe someday she would be able to meet the baby she brought into this world.   —Bryan

Our Final Letter to Lois

January, 1, 2009

Dear Lois,

Where do we even begin? Eighteen years ago the miracle of our family began when you selflessly entrusted us to become Mali's parents; she grew under your heart and into ours. God's plan for her life and ours has been a most rewarding journey. To merely say "thank you" could not come close to the appreciation and love that we have for you. To have chosen life for Mali and then to have placed that life into our arms is a miracle that we have held precious to us always.

When we look at Mali now, we realize we must have blinked one too many times. Time has just slipped away, quicker than we could have ever imagined. The reality that she will be starting a new journey at college, on her own, seems so ironic; how could this little girl who was just born yesterday be ready to spread her wings? And yet we know that everything that God has poured into her has not come back empty; she is an amazing young woman, ready to face the challenges in life that lay ahead of her.

So many wonderful achievements, activities, and goals were realized this past year. The fact that we've all kept up has been amazing! So many things to share:

Music: She has found her niche with singing! She continues to be a praise and worship leader at her youth group and recently joined the praise and worship team at our church. She auditioned for the top choirs (madrigals and jazz) at school, so is now in three, her senior year.

110

They will travel to St. Louis this spring for a tour; she is very excited! She is also part of the spring musical this year in the chorus. She hopes to be involved with music at whichever school she attends next year. Her first choice college has internationally known choirs that travel the world, so, we'll see where God takes her in that journey.

Children: This is by far one of her spiritual gifts from the Lord. She continues to surround herself with situations to be around children. She is still teaching Sunday School and added helping with our children's church choir as well. She continues to baby-sit and still enjoys it! This past summer, she was a camp counselor intern at a large Christian camp for a week. She was rewarded with a cabin of great girls who were seeking a deeper relationship with God; she loved being able to share her faith with them!

School: This is her third year on the yearbook staff and this year she is one of the Sr. editors. The staff had an award-winning book last year, which was quite an honor for them. She will be a part of the chorus for her spring musical and is excited to explore the drama department! She organized, for the third year, See You at the Pole, which is an annual national school prayer campaign where students pray around their flagpole before school. She is still on honor roll and National Honor Society and has now applied to four Christian colleges (as of today she has been accepted to two so far). Her goal has changed from elementary education, to either Christian youth ministry or Christian youth counseling. She has selected these colleges to help support her goal of being in Christian service. We are excited to see what plans God has for her future!

Work: After a job switch, she is now in a cookie shop, making and selling cookies. It is a limited part time job, but allows her to be involved with school activities and still earn enough money to cover her social life and gas!

Trips/vacations: Mission trip # 4 to Mexico was in April. We had yet another amazing year. Mali was in the midst of the children – right where God has always placed her. Her love for our friends down there, many of whom we have known for a few years now, runs so deep. We recently got back from another Florida vacation. We had a short visit to Disney World with Karen's folks and then on to their condo near the beach. We had a fantastic time and Mali still wanted to (and did) wait in line to see Winnie the Pooh!

Lois, you probably noticed a very definite time, when Mali was about three, when our letters started to show that God was really working in our lives. Since this is our last letter, we thought that the best way that we could express our feelings for you was to share with you where the last fifteen years have led us in our faith.

We were invited to a Bible study shortly after we moved in '94. We thought it would be a good idea to go to meet new people and to get to know church history. What we didn't realize is that those were the things that led us to going, but ultimately it was God that we met for the first time in a way that we didn't know Him before. We came to learn that the religion that we had followed was not the link that provided us with salvation to heaven for eternity. Rather, as John states in John 3:3 (NIV), "In reply Jesus declared, 'I tell you the truth, no one can see the kingdom of God unless he is born again.'" We learned that we must be born again in order to enter the kingdom of God and that can only be through a heart-felt belief in Jesus Christ. We learned that we are all sinners and that God sent his Son to take all the sin of *the world upon Himself; once we believe and accept that in faith, in our hearts, we have the assurance of eternal life. Previous to understanding the Bible, we thought our religion, church attendance, good deeds, etc. were the deciding factors and that in the end the scales would tip in our favor. We found, through years of Bible study, that is not the case.*

Our prayer, for you Lois, is that you have seen the faith journey that our family has been on in the past fifteen years. Mali's life is a living testament to God's love; she lives and breathes her faith, without fear of anyone thinking ill of her. She stands up for Christ always, has committed (on her own) to living a pure life until marriage (with a ring that she always wears as her conviction), and wants to be in Christian service when she gets out of college. Mali accepted Christ when she was 8 years old. We'd like to share an excerpt of her story that she gave as part of one of her college application essays:

"I became a Christian when I was eight years of age. I was at a friend's sleepover party where her dad led a short devotion and asked if we wanted to have Jesus as our Lord and Savior. I said yes and we prayed together. That is only the short version; God is only beginning to work in my life. I know, for a fact, I am a Christian because I understand that man, although created in God's image, is sinful. I have repented of my sinfulness and have accepted Jesus as my Lord and Savior. He died on the cross to save us from our sins, rose from the dead, and is living today. The Bible says that Jesus is the Son of God and that He fulfilled all the prophecies from the Old Testament. The Bible also says that salvation cannot be earned because it is a gift that must be received and accepted. Jesus is my Lord and Savior; He directs my

life in the way it should go. I rely on the Word of God when I am down and often remember different verses I memorized in my grade school years that help me have peace of mind with the problem I am facing."

Mali is an amazing person. She has so many gifts, talents, and dreams and has a deep, deep love of the Lord. Entrusting this beautiful child to us was an act of kindness and love that changed our lives forever. Thank you for the gift you gave to our family; we believe that God put us together to fulfill a very special plan in all of our lives. We have seen how that plan has played out for us; we hope and pray that you have as well.

When we last saw each other, we had all agreed that it would be Mali's decision, when she turned eighteen, whether or not she wants to pursue contact with you. She has known about you and your family since she could understand our voices. Adoption has been as natural to her as the air she breathes. We want you to know that she is very secure in the person that she is and has never expressed any feelings of loneliness, incompleteness or anything negative about her adoption. She very much appreciates the sacrifice you made for her and has come to understand that she was chosen once by God and again by us. Having said that, we have one last request to make. Mali has known for a long time that it will become her decision when she turns 18. We do not know what that decision will be. We promise to support her, whichever way she chooses to go. If she chooses to make contact with you, we will help her in the process and would welcome the opportunity of seeing you again. Our request is that whatever she chooses, that her decision would be respected. This is the reason we did not feel it was right to meet a few years back as we had always *said it would be her decision after she turned 18. We will be reminding her of that this month and will guide her through any decisions she may make. Thank you so much for honoring whichever path she chooses.*

We love you and thank you from the bottom of our hearts. With both tears and with great joy and gratitude, we say goodbye and pray that our heavenly Father would continue to watch over you and your family.

Wishing you many blessings from Him and much love from us,

Tom and Karen

Our Final Letter to Ruth

June 1, 2011

Dear Ruth,

How do we even begin? Eighteen years ago our family was miraculously completed when you entrusted us to become Joe's parents. It doesn't seem possible that Joe's journey will soon be changing course as a young adult ready to be in the world. Yet God's plan for his life and ours has been a most rewarding journey that has prepared him for this time. A mere "thank you" doesn't come close to the appreciation that we have; you both chose life for Joe and then placed that life into our arms. The last eighteen years have been nothing short of a miracle to us!

The years have just slipped away, quicker than we could have ever imagined and now, in one week, Joe both graduated and turned 18 all at the same time! It just doesn't seem possible to us and yet we know that what our gracious Lord has poured into him has not come back empty and that he is ready to face the challenges in life that lay ahead of him.

What a year it's been...

School: Joe graduated with honors, having been on the honor roll for his entire high school career! We praise the Lord that Joe has done this well! He has particularly developed a passion for cooking, which may very well be a future career choice. For now, he has made a decision to attend a Bible College for at least a two-year Associates Degree in Biblical Studies. He then plans to enroll in a culinary program. We can only say that God has so obviously guided Joe's every step and has been in the midst of his schooling. It is exciting to see how far he has come and continues to go!

Music: Both in school choir and church choir, Joe has developed quite a voice and love for music. We are gently (probably well understated) encouraging him to pursue choir in college and join an ensemble group that travels during spring break. We are hoping he will follow our advice!

Work: After working for a sub shop for over a year, he recently made a switch to a fast food restaurant and is doing a variety of things. He loves it (and loves the money!). This is giving him a great foundation for a future in culinary, responsibility, and, of course, helping him to save up for his college expenses!

Faith: The Lord has blessed Joe with the ability to relate to children, so he serves in many youth-related areas in our church. From being an Awana leader, to being on the youth drama team, adult choir, nursery school volunteer and a monthly ministry at an AID's facility. His heart is service and, in particular, working with kids. He is looking forward to continuing with Awana while he is in college! We do want to make sure that you know that Joe is a born again believer having accepted faith in Christ at a young age. He is planning on using his Biblical degree and culinary degree to work with children – perhaps in a Christian camp setting.

Other: Driving, well let's just say it's an ongoing process! He had a speeding ticket and a couple of accidents since getting his license, so needless to say, things have had to slow down for him a bit and we think he is over the hurdle of being a new driver. It is normal for him to be gone more than here now (thus, a typical teenager!); but he still doesn't think it is "fair" that he won't get a car at college his first year!

We've seen this baby boy grow into a handsome young man, full of love for our Lord, and ready to take on the challenge of Bible College. We are in awe of what the Lord has done in his life and feel privileged to have been a part of this incredible journey. We can't say thank you enough, so please know that it is just a small token of what has been so huge in our lives.

As we reflect on this being the last letter, we are reminded of the choice that you made for Joe those years ago and can only stand amazed at what God did with that decision not only for Joe, but for us. Please know that Joe has always known about you and has always known that, just as he was chosen by God for His kingdom, that we also chose him. As with Mali, we have let both of them know that it will now be up to them, since they are now adults, to make their choices in life. If that choice includes finding their birth parents, we will fully support them through that process. We hope that you would understand that we ask that this decision be Joe's choice now and that he would be the one to either establish contact at the time he would choose to, or that his choice to not have contact would be honored by all of us.

Thank you for the gift you gave to our family; we believe that God put us together to fulfill a very special plan in all of our lives. We have seen how that plan has played out for us; we hope and pray that you have as well. With both tears and with great joy and gratitude, we say goodbye and pray that our heavenly Father would continue to watch over you.

In Him and with deep gratitude,

Tom and Karen

CHAPTER 13

The Reunion (Karen)

The first time we heard about Lois's cancer was from Tom's cousin Pat. She passed along the news to us so Mali would be aware of Lois's condition and be able to see her if she wanted to. I started following Lois's story on her CaringBridge website. My heart ached for Lois and her family.

We shared the news with Mali and Jason, her husband, and encouraged them to pray about seeing her before making a decision. Initially Mali wrote a letter to send to Lois, as she didn't feel it would be right to step into a situation that would draw attention to her rather than to Lois. As the days went on, I got a sense from the website that Lois's health was rapidly declining. I also saw Mali struggling to know the right thing to do; Mali has always been a people pleaser, and she doesn't like to disappoint anyone, so Lois's cancer weighed on her heart. On the one hand, she feels secure in who she is as an adopted child and doesn't feel the need to "find" something or someone to complete her, as she feels complete. On the other hand, she realized that time may be running out and that her opportunity to meet Lois may not last for much longer.

A couple of weeks later, Pat's daughter sent a Facebook message to our family to inform Mali of the urgency of the situation and to find out whether we would be willing to talk with Bryan. With an open heart we gladly said we would. I remember listening to the conversation between Tom and Bryan; my godly husband was trying to encourage Bryan and, at the same time, let him know how special his mother was to us. When I had the opportunity to speak with him, it was hard to choke back the tears of emotion. Lois was, and continues to be, an extremely important person to us, and all the emotions of Mali's adoption came flooding back.

Bryan reported that Lois was in her final days of life. Lois had requested to see Mali before she passed. Both Bryan and Jenaya expressed their understanding that this was Mali's decision and that they didn't want her to feel pressured to meet with Lois, but they wanted to make sure she knew.

The next couple of days were a whirlwind of conversations, prayer, and emotional ups and downs, primarily for Mali. I can honestly say that we hoped she would decide to see Lois, but this decision wasn't about us; it was about her. It was hard to see the emotion in Mali. I think part of her hesitation was her desire to protect us; that's our girl … She's always putting others' feelings before her own. The other struggle came because she is so sure of who she is that this reunion hadn't been in her plans, but clearly as the hours unfolded, it was in God's. As is always Mali's normal process, she (and Jason) prayed and put the situation in God's hands; then, when they felt God's answer to go see Lois, that's the path they followed.

I'm so grateful that Bryan, Jenaya, Mali, and Jason invited us along. What a beautiful circle of our life story; we had come with empty arms twenty-two years before, and Lois had filled them for us with Mali. Now we were coming back to Lois with Mali to fulfill her dream before she left this earth. It was a small act in comparison, but we were so blessed to be on this part of the journey.

By the time we got to her, Lois was already in a semiconscious state. I clearly believe she knew what was happening that day. I held her hand, gave her a kiss, and with a very broken voice thanked her for the gift of our daughter—hers by birth and ours by adoption. I was so happy to share Mali with her, and I knew she was the only other person in this entire world (short of Tom, of course) who could understand the enormity of this exchange. She'd brought our daughter into this world so we could take Mali through this world; now, at the end of Lois's journey, we could share Mali together. I saw the smile on Lois's face. I felt the squeeze of her hand and knew she was aware of what was happening. Lois's sister, who had been with us at Mali's birth, was also there that day to share in the celebration of life.

Mali struggled with what to say to this person she really didn't know yet for whom she was so grateful. I heard her read her letter to Lois, filled with her faith journey. It was a beautiful moment. Mali later described parts of the day as being in a fishbowl; everyone knew a lot about her, but she knew very little about them. Then "the book" came out …, a photo album filled with our letters and the pictures we'd sent to Lois each year. I was so humbled that these yearly updates had formed a sacred tradition for this wonderful family. I was reminded that day of the importance of keeping promises and also the weight words can have.

Despite this very emotional day, I have to admit that there was a twang of jealousy; interestingly, Joe had the same feelings.

> When Mali decided to meet Lois, I had a lot of concerns. I wasn't sure where the reunion would lead to. I wasn't sure if there would be "sides" (where Mali would choose her birth family or her adoptive family). I was concerned about rejection for Mali.
>
> What I've come to find is that Bryan and Jenaya have been very accepting of our family; everything worked out better than what we thought and I like having a relationship with them. I have not felt any jealousy that Mali has met her birth family and I have not. Possibly finding them is still a curiosity,

> but my sister recently gave me some advice. She
> suggested that I not look for my biological parents
> if I'm looking to fill a void in my life.

The same fears I'd had early on in our adoptions came back. Would Mali form bonds with them? Ironically the answer to that was a resounding yes, but the bonds included all of us. I saw Jenaya's excitement as she showed us pictures of their life growing up; I remember seeing early pictures of her or Lois, who looked remarkably like Mali. I saw Bryan's sweet smile as he saw Mali interact with his mom. Dave, Lois's husband, and Lora, her sister, made us feel welcome. I saw all of them in pain; they knew that this wonderful person, who was so dear to them, would be leaving them soon. But they were happy that they were able to meet the missing piece of their family. When they led us to a room filled with Lois's coveted cookie jar collection and asked both Mali and me to pick one out as a remembrance of Lois, their thoughtfulness warmed my heart. From that point forward, they were part of our family, and we of theirs.

To see Jenaya and Mali next to each other, with the close resemblance they share, is to understand that our God is a great God, who weaves a tapestry of life together that is unpredictable and yet wonderful. Since that first reunion, we've been blessed to meet Jenaya's husband, Jesse, as well as her and Bryan's children. Our family is much bigger now, and we have made plans to continue meeting. What I couldn't see happening, God could.

> I know, without a doubt, that my mother was
> happy with the decision she made and if she had
> to do it all over again she would not have changed
> anything or any of the people that were involved
> in the process. Tom and Karen kept every promise
> they made to my mother and for that we will always
> be indebted to this wonderful couple.

Before my mother died from lung cancer on December 9, 2012 I made a very scary phone call to a family friend who had been involved with the adoption process. I was trying to get in contact with Amalie's parents to let them know that my mother was not doing well and if Amalie wanted to see her, now would maybe be her only chance. I got a phone call late that night from a man I hold very dear to my heart. Tom, Amalie's dad, wanted to know every detail of what was going on and wanted to let us know that they wanted to come see Mom before she went to be with God.

Thankfully Amalie was able to see the woman that Jenaya and I called Mom before she died; and my sister and I got to meet our sister for the first time in person and not just on a Kodak picture! It was a reunion that we had all dreamed of, though we wished it would have happened under happier circumstances.

I am thankful for the many happy years that Tom, Karen, Amalie and Joe gave my family. When Karen and Amalie asked if we would be ok for this book to happen, we knew that it will help Amalie, her husband Jason, Joe, Tom and Karen…my sister and I didn't even have to think about it we said "yes." If Mom were alive she would have wanted us to do whatever we could to help make their lives as good as they made ours. It was just another way my wonderful mother could help her child, Amalie, and her family.   –Bryan

On November 27, 2012, our cousin contacted me, via Facebook. She left a plea asking Tom and Karen to get in touch with her about Lois, who had gone into hospice because of cancer. It was one of Lois' dying wishes to see Mali before she passed. After reading the message, I felt that God had a hand in the situation. Ultimately He is our creator and this may have been His plan all along. The day had come and this could possibly be the time when things would come full circle for both families.

So many thoughts and questions went through my mind; I was sorry that she was suffering; wondering how her children were doing, knowing personally how it feels to lose a parent. Will Mali go see Lois? I was hoping she would but if she didn't that would be OK too. Mali's decision time was limited and I didn't want her to have any regrets. I felt myself wanting to protect her.

I relayed the message to Tom. This was a decision that Mali, Jason and her parents needed to make. All I could do is sit back and wait and pray that Mali would make the right decision for herself. Mali chose to make the trip along with Jason, Tom and Karen to Wisconsin to visit her biological family. I was hoping that the trip would go well, knowing that it would be emotional for all involved. I felt like I did when Mali was born. Waiting and wondering how everything was going.

I am glad that Mali chose to meet with Lois and family. I secretly was hoping she would. I knew that her bond with Tom, Karen and Joe was so good that they would conquer it together and there would never be anything that would change their relationship as a family. I have watched our family grow over the years and I am grateful that Lois gave our family such a treasure. Lois created a wonderful human being and Tom and Karen raised a lovely,

young woman. I am glad that I have been a part of
the experience.   —Liz

When Mali was considering meeting Lois, I
felt in my heart that she would. I didn't want her
to look in the rear view mirror someday with any
regrets. I know that her husband, Dad, and Mom
would be ok. I am very thankful to Lois and Ruth
for my grandchildren!   -Grandma Midge

As a family, we were honored to be reunited with Lois before
she died. For Tom and me, it was an opportunity to once again
thank her for the gift she had bestowed on us in creating our family
and bringing our daughter to us. Though Lois was in and out of
consciousness during our visit, we saw the smile that lit her face as
well as her occasional nods and the sense of peace that came from
her.

There were so many times over the years when we'd wished that
Lois could see Mali at a given point in time. And yet we believe
(and still do) that God always controls the timing of every event
that happens in this life, so He had already planned the events that
would lead to this reunion. As I recently told Jenaya and Bryan,
Lois's decision over twenty-three years ago is a testament to how one
person can affect many, many lives. Lois's choice to place Amalie
with us had done exactly that; it had affected many, many lives, and
it continues to do so now through the pages of this book.

Shortly after Lois's death, Bryan and Jenaya asked Tom to write
a prayer for her memorial service. With great thought, prayer, and
love, this is what we sent to them.

On December 9, 2012 Lois met Jesus face to
face. Knowing how much she cared for her family
and friends with selfless love, we can be assured
that she would want us to know that Jesus is Lord.

Jesus said, "Greater love has no one than this; that one lay down his life for his friends." (John 15:13 NASB). Lois' life showed evidence of a woman who continually placed others needs in front of her own. Our family was blessed by her selflessness as she chose life for our precious daughter, Amalie, and then made the decision to gift her to our family. In the greatest sense, her decision blessed many people far and wide beyond anyone's imagination. Most definitely, all of you can relate to how her life of gracious sacrifice impacted you as well.

This reminds us of a person that came to this earth to lay His life down for His friends; Jesus Christ. God the Father sent his Son Jesus from heaven to earth to be sacrificed for His people. As it is written in Romans 14:11 (NASB): "As surely as I live, says the Lord, every knee will bow before me; every tongue will confess to God." And Jesus said in John 14:6 (NASB), "I am the way and the truth and the life. No one comes to the Father except through me."

Like Lois on December 9th, we will all stand before Jesus when we leave this life and shall review our life with Him. We need to give an account because we are all sinners helpless of God's wrath without the grace provided to us through Jesus. Lois showed us how to live here on earth and has gone before us to give an account to God. As we cling to Lois' memory and to each other let us realize our mortality and our need for forgiveness. "For the wages of sin is death, but the gift of God is eternal life in Christ Jesus our Lord." Romans 6:23 (NASB). The good news is that our Salvation comes only from God through His Son, Jesus Christ, who died on the cross for us all.

Heavenly Father, we ask that you bless Dave, Bryan, Jenaya and their family and friends with your abundant mercy and grace. We thank you for the gift of Lois to each one of us that knew her as wife, mother, daughter, sister, aunt, niece, cousin or friend. We thank you for the life lessons we learned in her willingness to share her life with us. Be with us at this time as we remember her and help us to remember you. We pray, Lord, that you would provide the peace of God, which transcends all understanding and that you will guard our hearts and our minds in Christ Jesus.

We pray all of this in the name of our Lord and Savior Jesus Christ. Amen!

Sent with our sympathy, affection and love,

Tom, Karen and Joe Schlindwein
Amalie and Jason Bowling

Chapter 14

The Reunion (Amalie)

I chose to meet Lois out of gratitude and respect for her and her family. I went into the "grand reunion" scared and anxious of what the outcome would be, and I feared that they would dislike me because I was the one who wasn't "part of their family." I also feared that they wouldn't respect or like my parents and that they might try to "take me back."

I was pleasantly surprised to find that all my fears and presuppositions were false. Lois, Bryan, Jenaya, Lora, and Dave were so respectful and loving, and they treated my husband, my parents and me as family. Coming into an environment where everyone knew me was a strange experience; I knew only my parents and my husband. It was almost like being in a fishbowl, and I was the new shiny fish that had just come from the pet store.

Meeting everyone was surreal. Lois, at this time, was on a hospital bed with little to no response when I spoke with her. She didn't recognize my name, Amalie, but when Jenaya introduced me as Krista, Lois had a *huge* smile on her face. I remember looking down at her where she lay on the bed and thinking that this was the woman who'd carried me for nine months and then placed me with my mom and dad, entrusting them to take care of me. This was the woman who shared my DNA, who had lived a whole life and wasn't just a heroine in a story. The persona I had given to her just became a reality.

In this reunion I gained a new chapter in the book of my family. Family, to me, is a group of people who share love as one unit. Since I was newly married, the concept of family was very fresh in my mind, as I'd just welcomed a whole new "side" of family into my life—Jason's family. God used Jason's family to prepare me for this new chapter. My small family unit had previously been my mom and dad, me, and my brother, Joe. We added my husband, Jason, and now Bryan and Jenaya, who are my "birth siblings." They, along with their families, are now part of my family. All this is to say that I added many new, special people into the little community I call my family.

Growing up with my brother, Joe, was wonderful. I am the oldest child not only of my immediate family but also of all the cousins and grandchildren. Joe and I are what you would call typical siblings. We fight, we laugh, and we live life together. We've always had a special bond because we share something unique—adoption. When we were younger, I fought for him and protected him, and he also had my back. We stick together. He is my brother, and I love him so much.

I always thought it would be really cool to have a sister to share clothes and shoes, to talk about boys, and to just have a "ready-made" girlfriend. I also thought it would be really neat to have an older brother, someone who could beat up the boys in my life who'd wronged me, someone to hide behind when I didn't want to be the oldest anymore. And in that "grand reunion," I gained an older sister *and* an older brother. I'm proud to say that Joe, Bryan, and Jenaya (and Jesse) are my siblings and part of my family. Bryan and Jenaya were there when I was born; they have shared with me about Lois's life and who she was. Because Lois wasn't in a good condition when I met her, I really didn't get to know her or even have a conversation with her. Bryan and Jenaya are bridging the gap of the persona and reality of Lois.

It was somewhat strange going into the reunion, not really knowing anything about Bryan and Jenaya, and walking out with these new people as part of my family. It was almost like meeting new friends, except they knew all about my childhood. To them I was the sister they'd known they had and had grown up reading about but hadn't seen. I was their missing piece to the three musketeers. The day we all met was fun; we laughed, we cried, and we picked at each other just like siblings do.

It was strange to meet people who look like me. I have always seen families in which the siblings looked alike, but I'd never pictured that I would have the same features as my sibling. Joe is taller and strongly built, whereas I'm petite. He has greenish-blue eyes, and I have brown eyes. He has straight, dark blond hair, and I have curly dark-brown hair. Physically, we are opposites. I remember people being very confused and thinking I was joking when I told them Joe was my brother. So, as you can imagine, it was weird to find someone with the same smile, nose, eyes, and hair color to match my own. It was a new experience. We took a few pictures that day, and looking back at them, you can see that we share the DNA that makes us siblings.

My husband commented on how strange it was to see another woman who looks like me and has the same mannerisms. In the study of "nurture versus nature," there are some things that are learned from one's environment, such as intelligence and style. Other things, including looks and mannerisms, are from one's nature. At this point nature became very noticeable.

The relationship that "started" on the day of the "grand reunion" was just the beginning. A year later, (Christmas 2013) our families met again. This time Joe, Jesse (Jenaya's husband), and all of Bryan and Jenaya's kids were together with us. We soon realized how similar Joe and Bryan were, and we enjoyed getting to know Jesse. I also met my nieces and nephews. The kids and I got along very well. At one point I remember Jenaya saying about her youngest, "She doesn't usually like or attach to people. I am extremely surprised she asked you to hold her, and she is clinging to you like this"—to which my mom responded, "Mali is the child whisperer. Kids flock to her."

Bryan's daughter made a beautiful bracelet for everyone in our family, which matched the few things she knew about us. Mine was brightly colored, a trait that matches me perfectly. What a fun experience to have more children call me "Aunt Mali." Family comes in all shapes and sizes; the relationship doesn't have to be by blood or marriage. It is a group of people who care about each other and share a common trait—love.

This is the letter I wrote to Lois and had the blessing of being able to read to her on the day we were reunited.

November 29, 2012

Dear Lois,

Hello!

I believe the last time you saw me you were handing me over to the most amazing people on this earth, my parents. I am writing to show my gratitude. I heard you are ill and I'm sorry to hear that. I pray that you are in good spirits and that you are doing the best you can.

Let me start off by saying what you did nearly 22 years ago was a huge blessing. You changed my life forever. You made the selfless choice of gifting me to my parents. Since then I have grown up to be a woman striving after my great Creator and a woman who loves her family. I'm adopted, twice. I am special because I get to understand love in a different way than most people.

I have had the privilege to have two amazing fathers. You know my dad, Tom, but I'm not sure that you have met my other dad, God. When I was about seven years old I was adopted into the family of Jesus Christ. I have devoted myself to follow after Him and listen to His plan for my life. This may sound a little silly to you, but I want to fill you in on the most important part of the life you let me live. I believe God created the entire world, including you and me, and when He created our world and everything around us he called it all "good". It was pleasing to Him because everything was perfect. When He created man, Adam and Eve, a serpent deceived them and they committed, what we call, a sin. This sin caused creation to be broken. When this happened God was unsatisfied and wanted to fix or repair what once was a perfect creation.

Because God loves His creation He sent his only son Jesus to take our place for the sin that we have committed. In the Bible it says "for the wages of sin is death" (Rom. 6:23, NIV) meaning no matter what we do to try to fix our sin (good works, being a good person, doing the right thing) we still deserve death for what we have done. But the good news is that God sent His Son as a replacement for us. Jesus took our place on the cross; He paid the debt that we owed so that we might live. I don't know about you, but I would have a hard time dying for something that I never did. Jesus was perfect; He had no sin in His life, yet His purpose was to die for our sins. Not only did He die on the cross but three days later He rose from the dead and is living today. When He died on the cross and rose again Jesus created a bridge that allows us to repair our broken relationship with God. God asks that we love, trust, and follow him and when we do that we are rewarded with eternal life in heaven.

God is a huge part of my life, and is the reason I do everything. I have been studying at a Bible college the past four years to prepare myself to work with children and youth. I have studied how to communicate in their language, teach, and organize. I have spent four years learning about and studying the Bible. I also met my husband at college; we got married this past summer. We hope to go into ministry together and teach youth about our Creator. I am thankful to you and my parents for loving me and explaining to me the wonderful part of my life, adoption. Because I have been so blessed through adoption in my life, I have a love for those who are adopted and I hurt for those babies that don't ever get a chance to live. If I had the opportunity, I would adopt or foster all the children I could and love them as much as my parents loved me. I want to educate people about how wonderful adoption is, not only how I was adopted, but spiritual adoption as well.

I guess the reason I am writing is to say thank you for making the choice to place me for adoption and giving me my parents. I am very happy and I pray you are as well. I pray for you often and thank God for you always. In this time when life seems so fragile, I pray that you find happiness and joy in the life you have lived and I pray you have hope. Thank you.

In Him Always,

Amalie

CHAPTER 15

What Family Really Means (Jason)

"Family" has always been an interesting term for me. When people ask me how many siblings I, Jason (Amalie's husband), have, I sometimes have to stop and think to make sure I have everyone included. If they ask me whether I'm the youngest or the oldest, my response is, "The youngest, the middle, and the only." Growing up, I had two sisters and a brother, all older than me. All my siblings are half siblings, but the word *half* was never in my vocabulary when it came to them. I now have a younger sister to add to the mix—again, a half sibling. My brother is married, so we throw in a sister-in-law, and my wife has a brother, so we add a brother-in law. None of this matters to me. This is my family. Period.

I have always had this mind-set. Proof of that is an exercise I was a part of in fourth or fifth grade, when our teacher wrote a list of numbers from two up to five plus on the chalkboard. We were learning about the census, as it was a census year, so we were asked to count up the members of our family and tally the sum under the corresponding number. We went up, one row at a time, to add our tallies to the appropriate box. A few children of single parents occupied the two category, but most fit into the typical family structure and were in the three to four range.

When it was my turn, I put a tally under the five-plus marker and sat back down without a thought. Most students were thinking of their immediate family, which is what the teacher intended; but I didn't. At this point there were probably four of us at home, but I counted my grandparents, my aunts and uncles, and my cousins—every single family member I could think of. If my teacher had asked me for a specific number, I probably would have said something like "fifty." My point in all this is that family means something very different to me than perhaps to others. This exercise provided a unique perspective when faced with the idea of adoption.

Of course, I'd heard the typical older-sibling taunts from those who tried to get to me by telling me I was adopted (which I am not, just for clarity), but I had never really given the topic much thought while growing up. The only exposure I had to fostering or adopting was a neighbor friend who was fostering a child (whom I believe she eventually adopted); this boy was always just her brother in my eyes. I didn't see him as a separate child occupying the same space as my friend.

My first real encounter with adoption was with one of my cousins. Technically Sharon is my second cousin because she is my mom's cousin. But again, the idea of family doesn't limit those terms. I was just a baby when she was reunited with her birth family (my family), but I talked to her about adoption multiple times. From her retelling she said that originally she'd sought us out for some of the concerns most people who were adopted worry about, such as health histories or other family traits that might be good to know. She had no idea that she would be gaining a whole second family, a family that cannot imagine life without her now that we have her. She remains close with her adoptive family, and they, too, have even become part of our family through her. Even though there is no technical relationship, I still call them cousins and consider them family. What started as a journey for answers from my cousin turned into a tremendous blessing for all of us. She has become a best friend to my mom, and I consider her to be more than just family, but a dear friend.

As a result, when I met my wife and learned she had been adopted, this news had no impact on my view of family. I don't see her family any differently than other family. When I met her mom and dad, I knew they were *her mom* and *her dad*. Some people make the mistake of calling Lois Mali's "real mom" and don't understand that she *has* a "real mom," whose name is Karen. That isn't to say we're not extremely grateful for the gift Lois gave to all of us with Amalie, but people seem to have a hard time understanding that families don't always look the same. It didn't take long after the meeting for Amalie to realize that she had a passion for adoption and that one day it was very likely that somehow we would be part of that world; we just had to figure out what that part would be.

My wife, Amalie, is very strong willed. When she sets her mind to something, she is laser targeted in on that thing. One of those things I learned very early in our relationship was that she had her family and that she was perfectly content with that. She had no intentions of seeking out her birth mother, and that was the end of the story. I fully supported her in this decision because I knew very well what family means, and it was very clear that she already had her family; she had her place in this world. She was loved, and it would take a mountain to move her on this topic.

We didn't see the mountain coming, but it was ready for us. Very early in our marriage, we learned that Lois was diagnosed with cancer. This news shook Mali a little in her conviction not to reach out but didn't crumble it completely. She wrestled very hard with what to do next, but as far as we knew, Lois was sick, but we didn't know exactly how long she had to live. Mali eventually decided to write her a letter because, above all else, she wanted to thank her, to tell her she was happy, and to tell her about Jesus. Even after writing this letter, she wasn't entirely convinced she was going to send it, but after wrestling with the idea for a while longer, she decided to do it.

It wasn't long after this (and prior to the letter being sent) that we learned Lois was on her final days; and if ever there was a time to see her, it was now. Since both Karen and Amalie have written about their experiences with this event, I will just give you some of my perspective. I wanted to be supportive of my wife no matter what she chose. I walked her through the thought process behind the decision, reminding her that she wouldn't get another chance, but on the other hand, she is perfectly content with the family she has. No matter what she decided to do, I was going to be right there with her every step of the way.

Eventually we decided to move ahead and meet Lois. We traveled up north to meet Lois and her husband, Bryan, and Jenaya and Lois's sister, who was helping to care for Lois while we were there visiting. (We learned when we got there that she had also been in the delivery room with Lois when Amalie was born, so it seemed fitting for her to be there.) While I was nervous, I cannot imagine how my wife was feeling. I was nervous for a few reasons. I was first hoping that Amalie would get along with Bryan and Jenaya and that the feelings presented would be positive ones. I was nervous that Bryan and Jenaya might be resentful of Amalie or that they might not see her as a part of their family. I was also nervous that they might see her as a part of their family and that Amalie wouldn't be ready or receptive to that. But mostly I was nervous because I knew Lois had cancer, and I had recently watched my grandmother succumb to cancer. I was afraid I wasn't going to be able to hold myself together and be strong for my wife.

As we pulled up, we met Bryan and Jenaya, and a lot of nerves were set at ease. I was able to keep it together and be strong for my wife, and she was able to interact with everyone and be the strong woman I knew her to be. Relationships were forged that day that continue on. Now, when asked how many siblings I have, I'm overjoyed to be able to include Jenaya, her husband, Jesse, along with Bryan in that count. That day I was able to hear so many perspectives on adoption and hear such a positive outcome from what so often can be a difficult and painful experience.

My wife and I left that day with a renewed passion for adoption. The adoption world not only ignited but also exploded in our hearts. We talked about what that would look like; fostering was an option that immediately came to mind. But the idea of just one or two kids isn't enough for us; we want more. We don't just want to be a pit stop for kids in the foster system; we want to be a home for kids without a home. We want to love those who haven't seen what unconditional love looks like. We want to fill a big house with kids and love them with our whole hearts. We want them to have their own space, where they can feel like they belong. We want to show them what it means to be a family. We know it isn't going to be easy, and there will be kids who don't want to be there, but that is where *unconditional* love comes in. We want to love all kids of all ages, experiences, and pasts.

This book has been a way for my wife and mother-in-law to share their story and thank an amazing woman who gave a gift no one else could give. But it is more than that. It is fuel for our passion to make something more than words.

At the time I am writing this, I am also engaged in the lengthy process of developing a not-for-profit organization to turn these desires into real actions. Our organization will have three main purposes. First, we want to make that house of our dreams a reality and open a group home to give those kids who need a home and a family just that. Second, we want to raise funds so we can assist those in the adoption process—not just financially but also through counseling and assistance from those who've been through the process. We can also help answer their questions and be friends to them. Finally, we want to engage in the community and educate them on adoption and on adoption as an option for those who may be struggling with an unwanted pregnancy or infertility.

Family is family, no matter how family members enter our lives. We long and pray for the day when we will have this organization in place and can put our passion into practice.

Chapter 16

Karen's Final Letters to Lois and Ruth

October 15, 2014

Dear Lois,

> *"For we will walk by faith, not by sight."*
> *—2 Corinthians 5:7 (NASB)*

I try to imagine sitting at a table with you, expressing all that has been welling up in my heart for so many years. As hard as I tried in our letters to articulate our deepest appreciation and gratitude for the gift of Amalie, I feel that I couldn't begin to come close. I now have a unique opportunity to share my heart with you so that the world can know of the incredible impact you had in my life and in the lives of so many.

Picture a young woman who is devastated by being unable to conceive a baby and then faces a miscarriage after years of disappointment. She is lost, has given up faith, and feels her empty arms may never be filled with the baby she longs for so deeply. At the very lowest point of her journey, you, Lois, enter our world. Your first question stuns me. You ask if we will be in the delivery *room with you. My head is spinning; how could this stranger who doesn't even know us already be planning the delivery of her baby? It makes no sense to me; it makes no sense to us. You ease us into conversation; you answer our list of questions, and you wait expectantly, as if you already know what our answer will be, should be. Instead, we drive away, uncommitted to accepting this gift. Confusion explodes ... fears ... Will she change her mind? And yet you seem very solid in your resolve for us to raise this baby.*

Then God ... Then God. He reminds Tom and me both that we are receiving a gift and that this was designed for us, and yes, this is the gift we need to accept. We call with the news; you seem so happy and relieved. We still don't understand ... Maybe one day we will.

We scurry ... scurry to find an adoption agency, complete the adoption process (no small feat since you let us know this baby is already overdue), scurry to make our home ready for a baby. Rushing, running, shopping, home studies; so much to do. We are vaguely aware that our dreams are about to come true and yet ... Will something happen? Again? Will we walk away with the same empty arms that can never seem to be filled with the baby we so desperately want to love?

At long last, the day of our baby's birth (ours meaning yours and ours ... jointly—together); a day that we longed for and didn't know when, or if, it would ever come. You seem the epitome of calm. You engage us; you talk with us, even through intense labor. You even let my crazy husband push around an empty wheelchair, ready to catch you if you fall. You allow us to be so much a part of the birth that, short of pushing her out myself, I could have done no more to be involved. I cherish that gift, Lois. I value the experience we had to be able to

141

be a part of every second of her birthday. You didn't have to allow that, and yet you did—an event that was so intimate and so personal, and you allowed us in so lovingly and kindly. You put our needs over your own. I am in awe. I believe you wanted this child to know that her parents (all of us) brought her into this world together. What a blessing!

You insisted that we both see her entrance into this world. It was one of the most incredible experiences of my life. This priceless treasure that you bestowed to us was here ... a daughter—a beautiful, perfect daughter. All in that one moment, my heart developed a capacity to love this little human being beyond what I had dreamed and hoped for. I was instantly in love with her and so awestruck that this, the dream I'd wished for for so long, was coming true. That night we had our doubts ... Would you bond with her and not be able to let her go? Would Bryan and Jenaya beg you to bring her home? Would your family convince you that this wasn't the right thing to do? These questions ran through our heads. We held on to each other and hoped that this baby would come home with us the next day.

I truly didn't understand how you could find the strength to let us walk away with her, but you did. That day you picked her up and placed her in our arms and told us to love her and to have a good life with her, and you walked away. Many would say that you gave her up, that you walked away from her. We say that you loved her so much that you set aside your needs and found a way to love us enough to trust us to raise her. I believe God worked on your heart and gave you a peace to make your decision ...

My life has utterly changed since that day. I eventually found my faith and my passion, and I have *tried to help others along my journey. I learned that lesson from you. I have never helped people to gain favor or for any reward, just as you so graciously helped us. All the days of my life I will be indebted to you for our dear Amalie. I say "our" because she is the life that you created and nurtured and then we all brought her into the world together; then Tom and I were blessed to raise her — and to love her.*

I now understand how important the pictures and letters we sent to you over those years were to you. I am so glad. I wondered all the years of writing them how you would receive them. It turns out that you received them somewhat how I dreamed you would … as a family event … with your family by your side, excitedly watching her grow up. I know that when those letters ended, it must have broken your heart; I know it broke mine to write that last letter. I so much appreciate your willingness to allow Mali to come full circle in making the decision that we all allowed for her to make.

I now understand, I believe, how you made the decision that you did. As I have had the joy of parenting my two children, I truly understand what it means to die to myself and live for them. There is little that I wouldn't do for Mali and Joe if I thought it was the best thing for them. Putting their needs over self becomes natural … Having strength to hold fast to those decisions can be a struggle, but when done with love, it can be done.

Your decision over twenty-three years ago lives on in the lives of so many people. That one choice that you made has affected more people than you could have ever dreamed. I believe that you had many dreams for her; I hope we were able to help you fulfill them.

When I found my relationship with Christ, I learned that His selfless love caused Him to send His Son to die for me. I believe that He gave you a similar strength to allow you to share your child with us. Thank you, Lois, for touching our lives, and thank you for fulfilling our dreams!

With love and deepest gratitude,

Karen

October 15, 2014

Dear Ruth,

I have a Maker.
He formed my heart.
Before even time began,
My life was in His hands.
He knows my name.
He knows my every thought.
He sees each tear that falls
And hears me when I call.
("He Knows My Name" by Paul Baloche).

I wanted to publicly express to you the joy that you have brought to our lives because of your choice to gift Joseph to us! That one single decision you made changed the course of our lives forever. I do not know if we will ever meet again or where you are at in your life or even if you are still on this earth, but I am writing to allow my heart to share with you.

When we first met you and Wes, we had our two-year-old Mali in tow after recently having a five-month adoption journey end with a very young birth mother who chose to parent her child. Trust was very difficult for us at that point in time; we'd had so much pain and disappointment before Mali was born. You and Wes made it clear to us that you had chosen an adoption plan but that you did feel you had a choice to select adoptive parents for your baby, and it was important to you to be able to do that. We, of course, were overjoyed when you selected us. Could it be that twice in our lifetime God allowed a miracle to fall into our laps? How could this happen to us yet again?

As with Mali, we went into overdrive! Completing the adoption process... home studies... Preparing for another birth! Fortunately, we had a couple more months than we did with Mali, so we appreciated the somewhat-less-frenzied-yet-just-as-exciting journey! During our meetings with you over those months, we got to know about you and your family ... We used these valuable pieces of information to raise Joe, so those were life-impacting meetings for us.

Then came the day. This time we had to drive a few states over to make sure we made it in time for the birth. It seemed that the car couldn't go fast enough to get there. Just as with Lois, you were overdue, which was certainly God's timing, considering this wasn't your first birth! Despite the hospital's not embracing our adoption plan as we had all hoped, you helped us to make it the best it could be. Even though you were put in the hallway and then in a room so small two people could barely move, you didn't complain; how amazing that was and how brave you were!

We were so humbled that you allowed us to once again have the same experience of seeing our child born into this world—a son. We hoped for a girl and boy, and God honored that wish, too ... We held him for the first time and knew our family had now come full circle ... This was meant to be. There were no words to describe the sheer joy we had because of this little boy who was born into our family.

Over the next few days at the hospital, we thought there were a few times when you were going to change your mind. Who could blame you? He was such a sweet baby: so beautiful, so perfect. But you, too, found the resolve to allow us to take him home and love him. When you called us a couple of days later, wanting to meet us again, we were so sure you had changed your mind. I couldn't hold Joe, as I feared he wouldn't be coming home with us again. We were so surprised and so relieved that you both wanted to see him once more, just wanting to share him with your family.

I want you to know that I made a promise to Joe when he was born. I promised him that no matter what happened in life, I would make sure that I pushed him to do his best even when others gave up on him. He has had challenges in his life, but he has always managed to overcome them. I've kept that promise and will continue to do that until I have no more breath.

Thank you, Ruth, for your selfless gift to us and for allowing us to bring him into this world with you and then letting us love him and help him on through this life. Your decision, too, has impacted so many lives.

With love and appreciation,

Karen

CHAPTER 17

What Adoption Means to Amalie

Adoption is a beautifully difficult thing. To many, *adoption* is a word that is hard to grasp in our world today; in many situations it is frowned on. Those who are adopted often feel unwanted, weird, strange, or different in the context of family; it is challenging for everyone involved. The birth mother who places her child for adoption and cuts the ties of motherhood does something few women could imagine. The magnitude of love these women have by placing their child for adoption is unimaginable.

Adoptive families commonly go through so much in order to adopt. Sometimes their reasons to adopt are because they are infertile or single, or maybe they even tried to adopt before, but the birth mother changed her mind. Adoption is challenging not only for those women and families but also for the children. Each adopted child is different, just as each mother is different. But the adopted child may experience feelings of loneliness, confusion about who he or she is, or separation—which is common.

Thinking about adoption from the standpoint of adopted children, comfortable with who they are, there could be nothing better than adoption. Those children know their birth mother loved them and wanted a good home for them; hence, placing those children for adoption is a love for which they are grateful. These children know that their adoptive parents chose them to be part of their family and that no matter the circumstances these children will be loved unconditionally. I am one of those children.

I'm adopted. I was adopted straight from the delivery room. My parents, the family I live with, were unable to have children. They had been searching for a child to adopt for some time, and they finally came across my birth mother. My birth mother couldn't take care of me, so out of sheer love, she chose my parents to be my family. If I hadn't been part of my family, I wouldn't be writing this letter today.

Adoption is a beautiful thing; not only does it mean a child is placed into a family; it also means the child becomes one's own. I have family members who have made me one of their own as well as a heavenly Father who handpicked me to be His own. Have you heard of Him? His name is God. Did you know that God, too, placed His Son, Jesus, on earth to be part of Mary and Joseph's family? While Jesus was part of their family, He did some pretty amazing things. Jesus wasn't an ordinary child, since He was God's Son. While the Bible tells us all about Jesus's story, I'm going to share one part.

The Bible talks about how we all can be adopted into the family of Christ. It doesn't matter whether you already have an earthly family or whether you don't have any family at all; God loves each one of us. The Bible also shares some bad news; it says we're all sinners. What does that mean? It means we always miss the mark of being perfect, or we don't always follow the rules God has set through the Ten Commandments. Romans 6:23 (NIV) says, "For the wages of sin is death." This means if we don't follow the rules, there is a punishment for our sins (death), which should happen every time we miss the mark. But the Bible also tells us good news. Because we're all sinners, God sent His Son, Jesus, to take our place from the punishment we deserve to receive. Jesus died for us all on a cross so we don't have to suffer the punishment of death. Jesus not only died to save us from our own sins but also rose from the dead.

The news gets even better. The Bible tells us that we can be saved by having faith in Jesus Christ alone. Having faith means putting your whole trust in Him and believing that He died on the cross and rose again for your own sins. You may ask why you should put your trust in Jesus if you already go to church, are a good person, don't steal, and so forth. Those things are all good, but living a good life and going to church or doing good things aren't going to earn your way into heaven. You must simply trust in Jesus Christ alone, and then God (and only God) will give you eternal life with Him in His family. By placing your trust in Him, you are automatically adopted into the loving family of Christ. Adoption is a wonderful thing. God is the only Father who will continuously love you despite your sin if you place your trust in Him.

Is there anything keeping you from putting your trust in Him right now and becoming part of the family of Christ Jesus? Are you willing to accept the gift of love and adoption God places before you as you read this?

A NOTE FROM THE AUTHORS

For those of you who are still waiting for the day when your dreams of having a child are fulfilled, know that the Lord is walking with you on your journey. Know that He feels your pain, sees every tear that falls, and hears you when you call on His name. Whether you have conceived or miscarried, you have been, and are being, prepared to be parents. You have already given so much of yourselves for the sake of your future family, more than so many can understand. It is our prayer that you can draw on the love of Jesus to sustain your lives and that you can find joy in each day you live.

For those of you who have experienced the joy of having a child or children following infertility, our prayer is that the Lord will bless you and your family and that He will keep you in His constant care.

To any birth mothers who are anticipating an adoption plan to entrust their child's life with a waiting family or to those who have already made this decision, know that God is walking with you. You have made a decision that put your baby's needs over your own. For the decision you have made or are about to make, know that God is there and understands what is in your heart. Seek wise counsel if you struggle with your decision; don't walk this journey alone.

To adopted children, adoption can be confusing, lonely, and even frightening knowing there is another woman who gave birth to you but isn't the mom you've known and loved all your life. You're not alone; adoption is much more common than you may think.

Adoption is everywhere. Find someone to talk to about your fears and concerns. If you don't know Jesus as your Lord and Savior, seek Him and ask questions. Find your identity—not in being adopted or different but in being who you are. My identity (Amalie) is in being a daughter of the Most High King, Jesus Christ.

Adoption is exciting and wonderful. There are so many great reasons adoption is an option built on love. Love is the root of adoption; your birth mother loved you *so* much that she wanted you to have the best life possible. There are so many different ways a parent loves a child; look for those reasons in your parents. You may not look like your parents or talk the same language, but they chose you. You were chosen to be part of their family. They took you in as their own, which is the very definition of adoption. You aren't always going to get along or agree with them, but that's how family works. Be excited to be part of your *forever* family, because your *forever* family is excited that you're part of them. Seek someone to talk to and don't give up until your voice is heard. Always remember: you are never alone.

Coming Soon: Chosen

Chosen will be a ministry that hopes to create a loving, safe, and educational environment for children to see what a family really is. Jason and Amalie are praying that God will open hearts and doors for this ministry to form. With Chosen Jason and Amalie want to have a foster home that will have the ability to serve and love many children. They want to welcome and encourage kids who are hurting and broken, kids who need someone to love them, and to provide a place to call home. Jason and Amalie also hope to have an adoption ministry that will help connect adoptive parents with their chosen children. They want to help facilitate healthy, loving relationships between adoptive parents, birth parents, and children.

Finally, Chosen hopes to educate people about adoption through going out in the community and talking with people in schools, churches, and other public venues. Please be in prayer for Chosen. Pray for direction, funding, and the hearts of all the people Chosen will serve. Pray for Jason and Amalie to stay strong, because this road won't be easy, but it will be rewarding to see God in the middle of it all. We are excited to see how God uses *Dear Lois* and Chosen to impact the lives of many people.

To receive more information and stay connected to Chosen, please visit our Facebook page: http://www.Facebook.com/OurChosenFamily.

July 26, 2014

Printed in the United States
By Bookmasters